THE KOREAN WAR TRIVIA BOOK

Interesting Stories and Random Facts
From The Korean War

Trivia War Books Vol. 4

BY
BILL O'NEILL

ISBN: 978-1-64845-014-3

DON'T FORGET YOUR FREE BOOKS

GET THEM FOR FREE ON
WWW.TRIVIABILL.COM

CONTENTS

CHAPTER SIX: THE LEGACY OF THE
KOREAN WAR... 129

INTRODUCTION

Have you opened up Twitter recently and seen Donald Trump making some wild and insulting comment about North Korea? Have you asked yourself how he's getting away with this – or what North Korea might have done to be attacked so harshly? Do you wonder how, in 2017, there can be a communist dictatorship that doesn't allow its citizens to access the internet? If you have, this book is for you.

The Korean War is not one of the most popular historical wars. It's not the backdrop for hundreds of movies like the Vietnam War or World War II. No one dresses up in Korean War gear and re-enacts Korean War battles like they do for the Revolutionary War or the American Civil War. The Korean War isn't a big part of American history textbooks, and you might not even have learned about it once in school, while many history classes in the United States cover the World Wars or the American Civil War every single year.

But that's not the biggest difference between the Korean War and all those other wars. The biggest difference is that the Korean War is still going on.

Many people don't know this, but North Korea and South Korea have a temporary armistice – and at any moment, without having to declare war again, fighting could break out. This means that the Korean War holds a unique place in our culture – it happened long enough ago that it's history, but its effects are still ongoing that it's contemporary culture, too. That's why learning about the Korean War today is so important. It may be a seventy-year-old war, but it's still making an impact… and not a good one.

This book will help you bridge that divide between what happened in the 1950s and what's going on today. We'll start with some background, so that you have a good clear grasp on what was happening in Korea before the great communist-versus-capitalist war of ideologies split it in two. Then we'll examine the four main groups of players during the Korean War: the North Koreans, the South Koreans, the United States and United Nations, and the communist powers of the Soviet Union and China. By learning about all four of these different perspectives, you'll finish this book with a more rounded, more complex, and much more interesting understanding of what the Korean War really meant for the world.

Each chapter of this book contains fifteen short stories or explanations that will break down the complex, intertwined politics of the Korean War into bite-sized pieces. Some of these stories will introduce you to colorful characters, like Kurt Lee or John Thorton, while others will break down the politics and events of the war so that they're easy to follow.

The chapters will cover the actual period of fighting, from 1950 to 1953 (and the two years of negotiation afterwards), but they'll also look at what's been happening with each of our four major players since then, and what kind of imprint the Korean War has left on the world. More than perhaps any other war so far back in history, the Korean War needs to be understood as a part of the present, and when you learn about it, you should always be asking yourself – how are these events still affecting the world today?

At the end of each chapter is a quick list of twenty useful, interesting, or bizarre trivia facts, and five quiz questions that will test your knowledge! Get ready to impress your friends with your encyclopedic knowledge of both Korean War trivia, and genuinely complex politics.

So get ready to find out…

Did the American army really massacre Korean civilians like North Korea has said?

Which horse is hailed as an American war hero?

Why isn't the Korean War as popular a setting for movies as World War II?

How did beer bottles help defeat communism?

And much, much more!

CHAPTER ONE

PRELUDE TO THE KOREAN WAR

The Korean War didn't just pop up out of nowhere... it happened to a seriously destabilized country during a seriously unstable time. Korea had been under imperial rule for as long as anyone could remember, with just a brief blip of independence at the turn of the century, and when Japan was forced to surrender them at the end of World War II, both the Soviet Union and the United States thought that they were the perfect candidates for becoming influential players in the great communism-versus-capitalism divide that was tearing the world apart in the middle of the twentieth century. This chapter will introduce you to the history of Korea that made them such a vulnerable target for Soviet and American power plays, and also, exactly what kind of power plays the Soviet Union and United States were making in the late '40s anyway.

The Cold War

The Korean War was just one of a whole group of conflicts that were involved in the Cold War. The Cold War was a massive ideological conflict between capitalist countries, primarily the United States, and communist countries, primarily the Soviet Union (or USSR – Union of Soviet Socialist Republics – for short). The Korean War's role in the Cold War was overshadowed, a few years down the line, by the much longer Vietnam War, which cost many more American lives, and thus became a much bigger part of American culture. If you want to learn more about the details of the Cold War, and why the United States and the Soviet Union were in conflict, you can read our book on the Vietnam War, but here's a quick rundown.

After World War II, both the United States and the Soviet Union had gained next-level political and military power. They had access to nuclear weapons that could wipe whole countries off the face of the earth if they wanted to. And they had two completely different world views that, as far as the leaders were concerned, couldn't possibly coexist.

Neither side *wanted* aggressions to break out. Neither side *wanted* to end the world with atomic weapons. But more than that, neither side *wanted* the *other* side to end *their* part of the world first.

This led to the United States and the Soviet Union

taking out their aggression on each other in every imaginable way *except* actually declaring war. They competed to develop and show off new military technology, like the Soviet Union's *Sputnik*, which was the first human-made satellite. They spread propaganda among their citizens about the evils of the other side, leading to witch-hunts and rigged trials for suspected "sympathizers." And, most relevant to Korea, they had proxy wars.

What is a Proxy War?

Proxy wars are wars that are fought between two powers… but each of those powers is supported by another, bigger, power, and the beef between those two big powers is the real reason the war is going on.

During the Cold War, the United States and the Soviet Union had multiple proxy wars. By far the most famous one was the Vietnam War. There was the Greek Civil War, the Myanmar Conflict, and the Arab-Israeli Conflict (which is also still going on in the form of conflict between Israel and Pakistan). Virtually all of the dozens of proxy wars had a similar pattern: a capitalist country (often one that had, until recently, been under colonial rule by a western European power) tried to form a communist government. The United States (or another major capitalist power, but usually it was the United States) intervened on behalf of the capitalist status quo. The Soviet Union (or another major communist power, but usually it was the Soviet Union) intervened on behalf of the communist uprising. The two sides fought for a while, supplied with money, weapons, or troops from the major powers that were supporting them. Then, eventually, one side would win and usually install a dictator to prevent the other side from making a reappearance.

The Korean Empire's Big Dreams

But, of course, conflict in Korea didn't just pop into existence when it was convenient for the United States and the Soviet Union to use it as a proxy war. For decades, it had been experiencing all sorts of unrest.

In 1897, Korea declared its independence from China, which had held it as a "client kingdom" (a kingdom that's militarily subordinate to another kingdom) for centuries. China and Japan had spent a few decades sparring over it, and Korea was eager to both gain political independence, and to modernize its politics and industries. A series of reforms called the Gabo Reform were started in 1894, trying to get rid of some of the old-fashioned laws that were harming Korea. There were eleven key reforms: Korea became a sovereign country. The hierarchical class system was abolished. People of all social classes were permitted to study and be appointed to government. A new modern-style military and police force were formed. All official documents were changed into the modern

Korean script instead of the Chinese characters they had used before. Jobs that had previously been allowed to be performed only by "outcasts" (like acting and butchering) were no longer legally considered degrading work. The government's fiscal policy was updated, inspired by western industrial governments. The justice system was reformed so that witnesses and suspects in crimes were no longer allowed to be tortured, and no one could be arrested for being related to a criminal. Merchants could no longer hold monopolies. All forms of slavery were abolished (only twenty years after the United States got around to it, remember!). And child marriage was outlawed – men had to be at least twenty, and women had to be at least sixteen before they got married.

In 1897, King Gojong sealed the deal on not being part of China anymore. He declared that it was the beginning of a new era, which he called the *Gwangmu* era, meaning "warrior of light."

The Gwangmu era meant westernizing, globalizing, and urbanizing. This world order of the late nineteenth century was one where Britain was on top, industrial production was the way to get ahead, and western medicine and education were moving at breakneck speeds. Both China and Japan were pretty tentative about getting involved with the western superpowers, but Korea was interested. Their new reforms catapulted them into the modern age. They embraced modern western medicine (which had been figuring out how to get rid of exciting new things like germs and contagions, and so, unlike a hundred years previously, was actually a pretty big step up from traditional medicine). They also became very interested in education, and girls were allowed to be educated, which they previously had not been. This cultural value for education is still present in Korea.

The Korean Empire Didn't Last Long

Things were looking great for Korea. Their reforms were comprehensive, but not so radical that they picked up a lot of internal resistance. It looked like Korea was on the way to becoming a well-structured, successful country on the world stage – and without even getting colonized by Western Europe!

But things were not that simple. Japan wasn't thrilled about the fact that they weren't grabbing power anymore, and they were supported by major international powers. The United States president Howard Taft said that Japan having control over Korea would "contribute to permanent peace in the Far East" – no matter how Korea felt about it. Britain was also more interested in protecting Japan's interests than Korea's, and had an alliance dating back to 1902, saying that they thought it was okay for Japan to annex Korea. And without either the United States or Britain recognizing it as a sovereign country, the Korean

Empire's days were numbered.

In August 1910, Japan annexed Korea by forcing them to sign a treaty that deprived Koreans of control over their internal and international affairs. The Japanese government and political commentators predicted that Koreans wouldn't have much problem assimilating into Japanese society – after all, they had only been independent for about a decade, not nearly long enough to develop their own interests… right?

Japanese Imperial Rule

So, starting in 1910, Korea was back to being a property of Japan, and now, Japan really wanted Korea to be assimilated into Japan. They encouraged Japanese people to settle in Korea, especially farmers and rural workers, so that Japan wouldn't get too overpopulated. They also reformed land ownership claims – traditionally, land in Korea had been held based on who had worked on it the longest, but the Japanese wanted to turn to a system where you needed to have written proof of ownership. Slowly, more and more of the farmable land ended up in Japanese hands. Japanese landlords would "hire" Korean tenant farmers to work on the land they acquired – and "hire" is in quotation marks because they weren't really paid. In fact, they sometimes had to pay half their crops or more just for rent.

Life was rough for Korean people under Japanese rule.

Many women were sold into prostitution, or forced to work in factories, just to make enough money to support their farms. In 1911, the government forbid Koreans from taking Japanese names, making it easy to discriminate against them – and then, in 1939, the Japanese changed its technique entirely and *forced* Koreans to adopt Japanese names and drop their Korean family names as an assimilation technique.

But as hard as it was for Koreans during the teens, twenties, and thirties, things got a whole lot worse when World War II broke out.

Korea in World War II

To the Japanese government, Korea seemed like the perfect tool for success in the war – the people were economically and politically distressed and would, they figured, be *thrilled* to get work contributing to the Japanese war effort. As a bonus, even though the Japanese government had spent the last three decades being pretty nasty to the Koreans, they could capitalize on Nazi ideas of racial unity and get Koreans in on the game by insisting that they were of the same race and needed to stand together against western Europe. Propaganda depicting "Japan-Korea teamwork" gained some popularity among the less economically depressed parts of Korea.

Koreans were brought in to work in war factories. While the conditions weren't as bad as some countries, thousands still died – about ten percent of all the Koreans brought in to work in factories, including thousands who were victims of the Hiroshima and Nagasaki bombings because they had been sent to factories in those areas.

Korean Independence!

When Japan surrendered in World War II in 1945, the Allied powers weren't the only ones who were happy – Korean forces rejoiced! As part of the surrender, the Japanese government had to relinquish all their rights to Korea. Since Japanese expansionism was a big part of the reason that they got involved in World War II at all, basically the first thing that the Allied powers wanted to do was sever all their ties to overseas colonies, including Korea.

But Korea hadn't been independent for over thirty years, and had only had a few years experience at running their own government. So, while they were finally granted status as an independent state, it seemed completely reasonable that some Allied troops would remain behind, in formerly occupied land, and help rebuild the government and infrastructure that had been damaged by the war, and by Japanese rule. This was the same technique that the same parties were using in Germany, and seemed to them like a good balance. The United States and the Soviet Union had been on the same side during World War II, but they had radically different politics, and splitting the "conquered" territory half-and-half seemed like the fairest deal to make sure that both sides were getting a bit of the expansionism that they both so desperately wanted.

Russia in Korea

Russia had a long connection with Korea – back before it even declared its independence in 1897, the Russian monarchy had had a significant presence in Korea. Russia had acknowledged the Japanese rule over Korea at the beginning of the century, and they had even talked about splitting Korea between them, but by the end of World War II, Soviet Russia was having none of it.

In 1945, the Soviet army took control of North Korea and snatched it out of the control of the Japanese government. The United States was advancing into the South, too, but at that point, the United States and the Soviet Union were still on the same side, and that seemed like a totally reasonable way to divide the responsibility for rebuilding the country. In fact, it was so totally reasonable that it also happened to be what they were doing with Germany – and look how great that was working out!

The Allied countries had a plan for moving Korea towards independence – four major countries, two communist and two capitalist, would spend five years jointly supervising it and rebuilding the government. This was called a trusteeship, and was designed to be very different from being "ruled" by other countries. Everything seemed like it was going to work out just fine.

Cho Man-sik and the Soviet Union

The Soviet Army set up camp in Pyongyang, which is now the capital of North Korea, and had already been occupied by multiple foreign governments. When the Soviet Union got there, they found that another man had already taken power there – a nationalist activist named Cho Man-sik. Cho had converted to Protestantism and became very interested in the British empire as a young man. He was inspired by Mahatma Ghandi's non-violent resistance to the British government in India, and promoted non-violent resistance to foreign regimes in Korea, too. His ultimate goal was an independent Korea.

At first, the Soviet Union liked the look of Cho. They were united in their opposition of Japanese rule, and they thought they could influence him. But Cho was as suspicious of them as he was of anyone else who tried to take over Korea, and he wasn't a big fan of communism, either. The Soviet Union didn't immediately oust him from power, but they were casting their eye around for a more communist-sympathetic, less independence-focussed leader to replace him, as soon as they could.

Resistance from Korea

The idea of waiting five years for independence, especially independence that was supposed to be granted by governments that had been completely okay with letting Japan forcibly annex Korea at the beginning of the century, didn't sit well with all the Koreans. They demanded freedom and independence immediately, insisting that they would be able to build a perfectly good country if everyone else would just *leave them alone for ten seconds to let them do it*. The frustration was palpable, and citizens marched in the streets to protest the trusteeship.

The one group that was really supportive of the trusteeship agreement? The Korean Communist Party. They were closely aligned with the Soviet Union's Communist Party, and were assured by the Soviet Union that they were going to be well taken care of, and that the Communist party would have a good chance of gaining power. They were sure that if Korea gained independence right away, their chance at political success would be ruined.

John R. Hodge

As okay as the United States had been with the idea of jointly ruling Korea alongside Britain, China, and the Soviet Union, when they got an inkling that the Soviet Union *might* be trying to make some kind of alliance with the Korean Communist Party to get them into power, they decided that they needed to make a decisive move, showing that the United States was *really* the ones who Korea should be *most* loyal to in this whole trusteeship deal. So John R. Hodge was sent to Korea to manage the affairs there.

Hodge had trained as a teacher at the Southern Illinois Teachers College, but got into the military midway through World War I. He fought in France in World War I and in the Pacific in World War II, and had about as many decorations as any soldier could get. He was experienced, had won awards for his bravery and skill, and knew a bit about the political situation in Asia. He seemed like the perfect man for the job.

Maybe there wasn't anyone who would have done better, but to say that Hodge improved the situation in Korea would be a flat-out lie. He refused to meet with delegates of the Provisional Government of the Republic of Korea, and, in fact, totally refused to acknowledge the People's Republic of Korea as a "real" government. Instead, he pushed hard for elections, no matter what the people of Korea had to say about it.

Rhee Syngman

Hodge was making it clear that the United States wasn't going to support anything they perceived as a communist-tainted regime. Instead, they threw their support behind the right-wing anti-communist Rhee Syngman, who insisted that it would be better for everyone if the United States kicked Britain, China, and Russia out of the equation, and worked alongside Korea (and *only* Korea) to establish a capitalist republic. Rhee was the first president of the Provisional Government of the Republic of Korea, and (once he finally got through to Hodge) became the Americans' "man on the inside." Most Americans didn't know much about Korea, and Rhee's politics looked comfortable and familiarly western to them.

Probably the United States' favorite thing about Rhee was that he had absolutely no tolerance for communists. He was like so many western politicians at the time; completely obsessed with crushing left-leaning political dissent. He arrested his opponents, and rumors abounded that he was executing them without trial. He and his government arrested and tortured people who were suspected of being part of the Korean Communist Party, and he became known as a dictator – to everyone except the ever-supportive United States, who were much more worried about the possibility of communism than that one of "their own men" might be doing bad things.

The Assassination of Lyuh Woo-hyung

Not every politician getting involved in Korea in the '40s was a hard-fisted political ideologue... just the ones who survived.

Lyuh Woo-hyung was a peace advocate with a centralist

political ideology. He rejected oppression and totalitarianism from both right-leaning and left-leaning governments, equally criticizing the Provisional Government of the Republic of Korea, and the Korean Communist Party, for their anti-freedom and anti-equality rhetorics. He insisted that Korean independence from foreign powers *and* reunification of the Soviet-influenced north and the America-influenced south was the only way for peace to exist in Asia, or in the world. And people – even politicians – from both North and South seemed to agree. They supported his demand for peace and mediation – he insisted that serious and thoughtful conversation between right wing and left wing politicians was the only way to find peace. They just didn't support his views enough to actually carry them out.

In July, 1947, Lyuh was assassinated by a radical right-wing refugee from North Korea, who seemed to believe that anything but the harshest sanctions on communism could prevent a communist dictatorship. His death was mourned by both the South and the North – but with him, the last hope of peace between the two halves of Korea died, as well.

The Border

As the conversation between right-wing Americans and left-wing Soviets became more and more destructive, and people less and less saw any way that this would end other than with war, the border between North and South Korea became more and more hardened.

Many people don't know this, but the border between North and South was actually the border that the Soviets and Americans agreed on when they were liberating Korea – they agreed that the Soviets would take care of everything north of the 38th parallel, and the Americans would take care of everything to the south. It seemed like a good idea when they were on the same side! It was never meant to be a permanent border, just a border of convenience, separating the areas that the two superpowers were responsible for.

But it quickly became clear that both sides were developing their own sense of identity that was quite separate from that of the other side. What's more, both sides were eager to claim that they (and they alone) were the true government for all of Korea. The other side, both sides claimed, was clearly nothing but a puppet government of a malicious western superpower with nothing but their own interests at heart (both sides were, of course, right about this). But how do you maintain diplomatic relationships between two governments that both think the other side is a fake government?

Answer: you go to war.

The Troops Withdraw

Even though they were waiting with bated breath for the other side to make a wrong move, neither the United States or the Soviet Union was *quite* ready for open hostilities to break out, and they *had* agreed to withdraw from Korea once a government was in place. And, well, by 1948, a government was in place. To be specific, two governments: the South Korea government, already accused of torturing and executing political dissidents, under the rule of Rhee Syngman. And the North Korea government, with a communist government headed up by Kim Il-sung. You may have heard of him.

Warily, with a communist government established but the threat of overthrow just a few miles south, the Soviet troops withdrew from Korea in 1948. Equally warily, with a capitalist system established but the threat of overthrow just a few miles north, the United States withdrew from Korea in 1949. And both sides waited to see what would happen next.

RANDOM FACTS

1. The first modern western hospital of the Korean Empire was established in 1885, and was called the Gwanghyewon Hospital. It was renamed Severance Hospital in 1904, after the director Oliver Avison acquired a hefty grant from Severance Oil to improve the hospital conditions. The real fun fact? One of our writers is Oliver Avison's great-great-great-granddaughter!

2. The annexation of Korea in the 1910 Japan-Korea Treaty was never actually signed by the Korean King Regent.

3. Korea had a nation-wide political protest against Japanese rule on March 1st, 1919. After that, although Japanese rule remained strict, some of the most racist laws against ethnic Koreans were relaxed.

4. The 1930s, a period of economic disaster all over the world, was actually a good time for many Koreans. The landlords who were forcing them to work their land and pay half their crops in rent went bankrupt, and many Koreans moved away to cities. The government even acknowledged that tenant farmer set-ups were bad for productivity, and started putting laws in place limiting the role

of landlords.

5. While the Japanese government was happy to have Koreans doing their factory work, they didn't really want them in their army. Working in the Imperial Japanese Army was very prestigious, and many Koreans did apply for it, with acceptance rates as low as 2%. Until the war started going really badly for Japan, that is – in 1944, they started drafting Korean men to try to buoy their sagging army.

6. More Korean women were involved in the army than Korean men... but not in any prestigious position. Korean women were "drafted" and forced to join the army as "comfort women" – sexual slaves for Japanese soldiers.

7. During World War II, a Korean soldier named Yang Kyoungjong became the only soldier to ever fight on three different sides of the war. He was conscripted into the Imperial Japanese Army, then captured by the Soviet Union and forced to fight as part of the Soviet Red Army, and *then* captured in eastern Ukraine and forced to fight in the *German* army in France. He then got captured by the British and Americans, but didn't have to fight for them – in part because he didn't speak English and no one in their armies spoke Korean!

8. But don't believe that the Koreans were completely

helpless at the mercy of Japanese rule! A Korean independence activist named Lee Bong-chang attempted to assassinate the Emperor Hirohito, the emperor of Japan during World War II, with a hand grenade. Unfortunately for Korea, he was captured and sentenced to death.

9. A famous Korean novelist wrote a novel called *Home,* which depicted the miserable conditions of Korean villages under Japanese rule, and told the story of a student trying to mobilize them to protest against their oppressors. The Japanese government banned this book, and all books published by left-leaning presses.

10. The most famous banned book publisher in Korea before World War II was the Korean Proletarian Artists' Federation, a serious socialist organization that sought to use Marxist ideas to help the people oppressed by Japanese rule. So long before the Soviets got involved, you could say that there was a strong press for communism (or at least socialism) in Korea.

11. Rhee Syngman was one of the only Korean politicians in the '40s who spoke fluent English, which was why he was able to exert so much influence over the Americans.

12. The reason he spoke English? When he was a young man, he had been an English instructor at a

missionary school, and a huge fan of the Enlightenment period of philosophy. Enlightenment thinkers, who included the American and French revolutionaries in the late 1700s, were the model for many of his political values and criticisms.

13. Rhee Syngman's birth name was Yi Sungman, and he "westernized" it to Sygnman Rhee (using the European style of putting the given name before the family name). In this book, we've preserved the Korean naming convention of putting the family name first, but used Rhee's westernized spelling.

14. Lyuh Woo-hyung was such a powerful figure advocating for peace that both North Korea *and* South Korea speak of him with great respect, even today… maybe the only politician who can say that.

15. In 1910, Lyuh freed all the slaves held by his household in a dramatic rejection of tradition and support of modernization. He believed in independence for everyone, including the enslaved.

16. A form of taekwondo was named after Cho Man-sik, but was removed from the Global Taekwan-do Federation's syllabus to avoid offending anybody by bringing an anti-communist North Korean into the discussion.

17. The same tactic that the Soviet Union and the United States were using in Korea – dividing the

territory up and having one side deal with each part of it – was the one that they were using in Germany. East Germany was being "reconstructed" by Soviet forces, while West Germany was being "reconstructed" by American forces.

18. The Soviet troops established their base in Pyongyang, while the American troops established their base in Seoul. These are still the capitals of North Korea and South Korea, respectively, even though the occupation ended decades ago.

19. Kim Il-Sung became the leader of North Korea under the Soviet Union, but North Korea has depicted him as a great leader against outside tyranny. North Korean biographies say that when he was a young man, he crossed out the Japanese titles of schoolbooks and rewrote them in Korean, showing the strength of his conviction to Korean identity.

20. It has become very important for North Korea to depict Kim Il-Sung as a hero and savior. We'll learn a lot more about him in the next chapter, but remember, starting now: North Korea's government has put a lot of work into creating the "myth" of the Korean War effort in general, and Kim Il-Sung in particular, so everything that you hear about him – just take it with a grain of salt.

Test Yourself – Questions and Answers

1. Who established the Korean Empire?
   a. King Gojung
   b. Lyuh Woo-hyung
   c. Kim Il-sung

2. What is a proxy war?

   a. A war carried out by attacking another country's proxy servers, thus limiting the flow of information
   b. A war that adopts the tactics of the famous Proxy army
   c. A war between two players, each one supported by a different, more powerful player, when the real major conflict is between the two more powerful players.

3. Where is the border between North and South Korea?

   a. The Pyongyang River
   b. The 38th Parallel
   c. The Pacific coast

4. Who was Cho Man-sik?

   a. A communist idealist inspired by Vladamir Lenin's politics
   b. A pre-communism North Korean leader inspired by Mahatma Ghandi's non-violent resistance tactics

   c. An American spy who worked for thirty years in the North Korean government

5. When did American troops withdraw from Korea?

   a. 1945

   b. 1949

   c. 1953

Answers

1. a
2. c
3. b
4. b
5. b

CHAPTER TWO
NORTH KOREA

North Korea. It's all over the news, and that's probably where you know the broad strokes of its situation from. Stories of human rights violations come out every week, its nuclear tests have the whole world on edge, and it's cut off from the rest of the world in a way no other modern country has managed. But how did it get that way? Before the Korean War, North Korea and South Korea were just two geographical regions of the same country – and even during and after the war, it took a while for Korea to transform into the dystopia it is today.

Communist Guerrillas

In the late '40s, right before the Soviet Union withdrew their troops from the Korean peninsula, there was an active communist guerrilla force making an impact on the South. The Soviet Union withdrew their support from these forces before they left, but Kim Il-sung, who had become the leader of the communist government established by the Soviet Union, was convinced that the guerrilla forces had a useful role to play. He firmly believed that the communist government that the North had established was a much better kind of government than the American-inspired capitalist system of the South, and he was sure that if he could just liberate the Southern people, they would welcome him. Because of this, Kim continued to support the remaining guerrillas, using them to tie up and weaken the South Korean military.

The word "guerrilla" comes from a Spanish word meaning "little war," and their tactics are an alternative to "traditional" warfare. Guerrilla forces are generally small groups with limited weapons, but their advantage comes from their familiarity with the terrain they're fighting on, and their ability to move quickly and launch surprise attacks. Guerrillas are the ideal forces when a small (or underfunded) military has to go up against a bigger military. Traditionally, guerrilla forces have represented rebellions, or the needs of the people, against a governmental military power.

The communist guerrilla forces of the years right before the Korean War broke out were small bands of Korean natives, and they focussed on taking out small bands of South Korean soldiers. Because they could easily disguise themselves as local civilians, with no one knowing the difference, these groups put the South Korean military on edge.

Why Go to War?

Not even a year after the Soviet Union withdrew their troops from North Korea, Kim Il-sung travelled to Moscow to seek Soviet support for a full-on invasion of South Korea. He argued that the only way to reunify Korea and bring peace was to invade the South, oust the American regime that was active there, and establish a communist government over the entire peninsula.

Kim had good reason to think that a communist government would be successful in Korea. After all, the two countries Korea bordered on – China and Russia – were both communist states. He was sure that they would both support him. He figured it would be a lot easier for North Korea to get troops and supplies from two states that bordered on it, than it would be for South Korea to get troops and supplies from the Americans, all the way across the Pacific Ocean, or the British or French, all the way across Europe and Asia. Besides, once the South Koreans saw how great communism was, they would welcome their North Korean rulers, even if it was *technically* an invasion.

Stalin's Opinion

Despite Kim's enthusiasm, Joseph Stalin, the leader of the Soviet Union, didn't think a war in Korea was such a great idea… in 1949. Just one year later, things had changed completely. In 1949, there were still American troops in South Korea, China was fighting a communist-versus-capitalist civil war that the Soviet Union had to support them in, and the Soviet Union still felt like they hadn't caught up to the Americans weapon-wise. Remember, in 1945, the United States dropped two atomic bombs on Japan, showing both that they had the technology to basically wipe an entire country off the map, and also that they were *definitely* okay with using it in Asia (they would *probably* be okay with using it in Europe, too, but *definitely* Asia – remember, this was a historical high point for straight-up racism). Stalin thought it would be stupid to start a war in Korea.

But in 1950, the United States had withdrawn from South Korea, Mao Zedong had fixed up the civil war in China and ensured a communist government there, and the Soviet Union had developed (and detonated) a nuclear bomb that could rival the Americans'. All those barriers to Soviet involvement were suddenly gone.

Even better, the United States had stood by and let a communist government take control of China. Stalin figured that this probably meant the United States didn't care *that* much about the spread of communism into Asia – if they weren't willing to do anything about a major power like China, why would they bother spending military energy on a tiny not-even-an-independent-country-yet country like Korea?

Perfect, Stalin decided. War was the way to go. It

would be a short war. Just a temporary invasion, really. With Soviet and Chinese support, establishing a unified communist government would be quick and easy.

Mao Zedong

Stalin had just one condition for supporting Kim's invasion into the South – he also had to get support from the communist Chinese Chairman Mao Zedong. Stalin didn't want to engage directly in combat, and figured that if Mao was offering support, too, *he* could supply the bodies while Stalin supplied the money.

Mao didn't have much choice but to go along with this. China didn't have the resources to fight a superpower like the United States – but they *definitely* didn't have the resources to operate as a communist country without the Soviet Union's help. The Soviet Union was providing troops, money, and protection to China, so if Stalin said he wanted Mao to support North Korea, then Mao was going to support North Korea. He met with Kim in the spring of 1950, and agreed to move an army towards the Korean border, ready to jump in and help when they were needed.

Conversations with South Korea

Kim was worried that the South Korean army had somehow found out about North Korea's plans to invade. We'll learn more about South Korea in the next chapter, but for now, it's important to know that they had been trained by the American military, and they were as ready to fight against communism as North Korea was ready to fight for it.

In June, 1950, Kim sent North Korean diplomats into the South to talk to Rhee Syngman. They didn't want a full-on war, they said. It would be much better for everyone if they could find a peaceful way to reunify... but that rang hollow when they had the Soviet Union's money and China's army ready to support them in an attack. Rhee didn't believe for a second that Kim had any intention of peaceful conversation.

Fine! Said Kim. If Rhee wasn't going to open the doors to political negotiation, then why would Kim go easy on him? Up until then, North Korea had been planning to start with a small attack on the Ongjin peninsula, more to show that they were willing to use force than anything else. But that wasn't good enough for Kim anymore. He changed his plan – and got ready to launch an attack all along the 38th parallel. That would show them! And if South Korea was already initiating skirmishes on the border... even better! That would just move things faster.

The Korean People's Army

Just what did the North Korean army look like? Well, first off, it wasn't actually called the North Korean army – it was called the Korean People's Army, or the

Chosuninmingun. It had its roots in the anti-Japanese guerrilla forces that came from way back when Korea was under Japanese control, and was made up of mainly volunteers. There was an official training school in China, but many of the people in the Korean People's Army were people who had been forced to fight in the Imperial Japanese army during the final years of World War II – especially ones who had deserted (ones who hadn't deserted were regarded with some suspicion).

The Soviet Union had ordered the Korean People's Army to disband while the territory was under Soviet control, but once North Korea was established as communist territory, the Soviet Union sent Soviet-trained Koreans around the country to re-establish forces – this time with Soviet-approved strategies.

When Stalin agreed to support the invasion of South Korea, he supplied the Korean People's Army with modern weapons that *way* outstripped what South Korea had access to. He provided them with tanks, trucks, and firearms – nothing that could take down, say, the United States army, but definitely enough to take care of the under-supplied South Korean army. The Korean People's Army had about 200,000 troops, and it's hard to say how many South Korea had, because they weren't even organized into troops for combat, yet. They had about 98,000 soldiers, which could have been as few as a couple hundred troops.

Even though North Korea's population was less than half that of South Korea, they clearly had the far better-prepared army, no matter what the Americans (who assured everyone that the South Korean army could take out the North Koreans, no problem) might believe.

July 25, 1950

It was first thing on Sunday morning, July 25th, 1950, when the Korean People's Army crossed the 38th parallel and officially invaded South Korea. They had multiple justifications for attacking – from claiming that the South Korean army had invaded first, to claiming they were going to execute Rhee Syngman as a traitor to the state. But it was obvious that this was the attack Kim had been planning from the start.

The first shots were fired at Ongjin, the original point that Kim had planned to invade, back before Rhee had spurned his diplomatic overtures, when they thought the invasion might be more symbolic than anything else. Within one hour, the entire 38th parallel was under North Korean attack, and without any supplies to deflect North Korea's heavy machinery attack, South Korea must have felt like there was no hope.

South Korean civilians fled further south from the border to avoid the incoming North Korean army, and the South Korean army, spread thin over the entire border and unprepared for such a decisive attack, struggled to hold their own against the invaders.

Help from China

As soon as they saw what North Korea was trying to do, the United Nations forbid China from getting involved. The UN took a distinctly pro-South Korea position that we'll read more about in the next two chapters, but China had already made their pact with North Korea and the Soviet Union, and now they had to uphold it.

The Premier, Zhou Enlai, made a statement to the UN on August 20th, 1950: "The Chinese people cannot but be concerned about a solution of the Korean question." With this statement of purpose, Zhou made it clear that China would not fight against their communist ally.

The president of the United States, Harry Truman, laughed off Zhou's statement. He called it "a bald attempt to blackmail the UN." He didn't believe for one second that China would *actually* do anything to oppose the UN's directives. On the very same day that the United Nations got together an army and crossed the 38th parallel into North Korea, both Stalin and Kim Il-sung sent messages to Zhou and Mao Zedong demanding that they send in troops to help, like they had promised.

Five days of intense political debates followed. Mao and Zhou were committed to intervening on behalf of North Korea, but none of their military commanders were too hooked on the idea. Not until a leader named

Peng Dehuai made a speech to the rest of the government, did he convince them. Peng argued that supporting North Korea was the only way to keep China and its new communist government in place. He argued that if the United Nations – and *especially* the United States – gained control of North Korea, their next step would be to take control of China, too. The only way China could stop that from happening was to act now, and act decisively.

Soviet Support

You may have already gotten the impression that Stalin was not super interested in actually putting himself or the Soviet Union's resources on the line to help the North Koreans. Although they had encouraged the conflict, and assured North Korea that they would support them with supplies and equipment (if not manpower), getting Stalin to follow through on that deal proved to be a real challenge. Zhou actually had to personally go to Stalin's home, just to get him to even *think* about offering any support, and even then, Stalin was evasive. He said they would sell China equipment on credit, but that they would want their money back eventually. He said they would lend their air force, but would only operate it in Chinese airspace (exactly what good that was supposed to do when they were fighting over Korea was deliberately unclear). He also said that he wouldn't send any equipment at all until next March (this conversation was happening in October). The Chinese government was frustrated, but Stalin was the biggest support they had, so they bit their tongue and agreed to his demands.

Spoiler: when the Soviet shipments of equipment finally did arrive, they were not very impressive. Stalin sure wasn't going to waste his nuclear arms or high-powered tanks on Korea. He sent them a handful of trucks, some grenades, and machine guns left over from World War II.

Kim Il-sung, and the Philosophy of Dictators

So, we've got the soldiers set up and the battles underway. We'll get back to the nitty-gritty of the fighting tactics and the anti-communist forces in the next two chapters, but for now, this is a good time to talk a bit about life in North Korea.

You can't talk at all about life in North Korea without talking about Kim Il-sung, and that's because he completely – and by design – *dominated* life in North Korea.

Up until now, we've talked about Kim in basically the same way that we've talked about other leaders and commanders. We've talked about how he got into his position, and what his tactics were. You now know that he was a communist leader with strong ties to the Soviet Union and China, and that he was committed to reunifying Korea under a communist government. But that really isn't the most important thing about Kim.

The thing about dictators is that their politics are kind of secondary. Sure, they matter because they're important to how the dictators come to power – if Kim Il-sung had been a fascist, or a libertarian, he would have had to use totally different tactics to gain power. So his communist principles got him to his position as Supreme Commander of the Democratic People's Republic of North Korea, but they weren't what mattered most once he was there.

What mattered most once he was there was the cult of personality that built up around him. His birthday was made a public holiday, called the Day of the Sun. He was titled "Eternal President of the Republic," meaning that his political power couldn't be limited by anything, not even his own death. And although North Korea isn't a monarchy, Kim Il-sung's son, Kim Jong-il, replaced him – and was eventually replaced by North Korea's current leader, Kim Jong-un.

No matter how many human rights abuses North Korea committed under Kim Il-sung's rulership, the North Korean literature surrounding him calls him a benevolent and loving ruler. Everything he did, he did for the best interests of the country. War crimes? What war crimes? His death from a heart attack was followed by a period of national mourning – and not just state-sanctioned mourning. As with so many dictators, the people who lived under them formed genuine attachments to their images. Of course, it can be really hard to tell how much of that feeling is genuine, and how much is just publically expressed, but one refugee tells the story of her grandmother breaking down in tears when she heard of the dictator's death. He was, she said, like a father.

Juche

Kim Il-sung promoted a philosophy of Korean patriotism and independence, called *Juche*. *Juche* is sometimes translated as self-reliance, but perhaps the more telling description is the official governmental definition: Juche is Kim Il-sung's "original, brilliant, and revolutionary contribution to national and international thought" (the idea of self-reliance is as old as foreign policy gets, so clearly it's not as simple as that), that "man is master of his destiny," and that North Koreans are the "masters of the revolution." This philosophy demands that North Korea, as a country, should not rely on any outside influence, and North Koreans, as people, should not rely on anyone else.

If you're finding this philosophy a little hard to square with either communist ideology, or North Korea's actions during the war (say, their reliance on China and the Soviet Union)... you're not wrong.

The idea was that this was a Korean "take" on

communism. After so many centuries of being ruled by other governments, Korea was very eager to be independent. The philosophy and religion of Confucianism that informed many aspects of Korean culture also emphasized self-reliance. It was a little different from the European communist idea of working-class unity, but it did favor the idea of banding together to overthrow people who would try to take away your independence, so the "worker's revolution" principle of Karl Marx's original communist writing was definitely there. But at the end of the day, nation-wide communist regimes require a powerful central government that will *always* limit people's ability to be "masters of their destiny." You can argue about the relative benefits and drawbacks of that central government, but it can never coexist with total personal independence. It just can't.

Besides, as we've just seen, North Korea was leaning heavily on both China and the Soviet Union for support of their war effort. How did they get around that? Well, that one was probably just some straight-up cognitive dissonance. It's easy for a powerful government – especially one that was okay with executing political dissenters – to get away with doing things that don't exactly go along with their stated ideologies.

The Sinchon Massacre, and the Sinchon Museum of American War Atrocities

One of the most famous examples of North Korean war propaganda is the Sinchon Museum of American War Atrocities, which was built in 2015 to commemorate the Sinchon Massacre. What exactly was the Sinchon Massacre? Good luck figuring it out. The North Korean government claims it was a massacre of about 35,000 people by the United States military. If this figure is correct, that would be about one quarter of the entire population of Sinchon – a town in the southern part of North Korea. Non-governmental North Korean organizations agree with these statements, and describe dozens of horrific torture tactics used by the Americans.

But their report has some holes in it. The report is based on oral testimony from North Korean survivors, but isn't confirmed by any photographic evidence… although the report claims that an American, General Harrison, oversaw and photographed the event. And that's another problem – no one named Harrison was in the area at the time, and General William Kelly Harrison, the prime suspect, *definitely* wasn't there. Of course, it could have been a pseudonym.

Other authors have claimed that there was a massacre, but that the American military wasn't there, and it was a South Korean tactic. Not that that really makes things any better, but Bruce Cumings argues, in his book *War and Television,* that Korean officials are very reluctant to attribute war crimes to other Koreans, even their enemies. He is aligned with sources that claim the massacre was the result of a local rivalry, and that the war was just a cover for an unrelated attack. We just don't know. But it squares much better with the North Korean narrative of Korean national unity to blame it on the United States.

And then there's the allegations of exactly what happened at the Sinchon massacre. It is absolutely true that massacres are rarely efficient or practical, and often involve bizarre and sadistic choices that seem hard to believe without the right context – and context is hard to come by when we're talking about North Korea. But North Korean textbooks allege that Americans "hammered nails into victims' heads," "sliced off women's breasts," and "beheaded civilians with Japanese samurai swords." Is it possible that these things happened? Of course. Is it so likely that it doesn't raise any questions at all? Not really.

Whether every allegation against the American army is true, whether not a single person in Sinchon was harmed, or something in between, we just don't know right now. What we do know is that the Sinchon Museum of American War Atrocities was not built to honor the dead – it was built to incite hatred against everyone outside of North Korea. It displays gory paintings of American soldiers torturing Korean civilians. The only photographs of the alleged attackers are blurry and from the back – nothing that would hold up as evidence if the event was being investigated as a war crime. The purpose of the Sinchon Museum of American War Atrocities is not to educate the public about history. The purpose is to paint the enemy as sadistic monsters, to frighten and sow hatred.

The Stalemate

One of the most shocking and tragic things about the Korean War is how little actually changed from the first months of the attack to the end of the active fighting period. Between July 1951, and July 1953, the North Korean army was coming into constant conflict with the South Korean, United States, and United Nations armies, but almost no territory changed hands. The division along the 38th parallel stayed the same, day after day, no matter how many people were killed. This entire period was known as "the Stalemate."

The Korean People's Army, under the leadership of Kim Il-sung and the North Korean government, spent this time trying to dissuade the South Koreans and aligned forces from continuing the war, using both military and psychological campaigns. They spread anti-government sentiment among the commoners, especially the ones living near the border, hoping that would encourage them to rise up against the South Korean army through guerrilla warfare. They also repeatedly launched what looked like peace campaigns, but were actually meant to further confuse and destabilize South Korea. Their entire plan was to turn South Korean opinion against their leaders and facilitate an easier defeat, so they could spread their ideology into the southern part of the country.

These tactics were no more effective than any of the many military campaigns. There were multiple battles along the 38th parallel, but although the rates of casualties were high, these campaigns typically didn't involve much exchange of territory, or any real advantage changing hands. The two Battles of Pork Chop Hill were especially controversial, because the territory that was being fought over wasn't even territory with any real strategic value. It was a conflict between the American and Chinese armies, and over a thousand Americans were wounded, while over one and a half thousand Chinese soldiers were killed and four thousand were wounded.

Visiting North Korea

Until this day, North Korea and South Korea are still technically at war – they never ended it. The entire carefully-planned state is under an insular communist regime that limits any civilian's contact with the outside world. What have these decades of carefully-controlled government propaganda done to the people of North Korea? Are they happy with their lives?

Despite the tight controls on movement in and out of North Korea, it is possible to go on an organized tour of the country – even as an individual traveler. In her memoir *My Holiday in North Korea, the Funniest/Worst Place On Earth*, Wendy E. Simmons describes her experience as a solo woman in the country.

The first thing about that: "solo" actually means carefully guarded by two North Korean tour guides, whose entire job is to keep the traveler from interacting too much with the locals, and to instill North Korean propaganda. Simmons' guides constantly praised the "dear great dead ones" Kim Il-sung and Kim Jong-il for their incredible wisdom and generosity, no matter how unwilling Simmons was to believe them. They also called her an "American imperialist" and told her that she was the reason that North and South Korea were not unified. According to Simmons, North Koreans truly want a unified state, like they had before the Korean War, and they believe that the only reason the Korean War happened and is still going on is that American imperialists are too attached to their hold on South Korea to let the country reunify under one "benevolent" communist government.

Americans are the Enemy

In 2016, Will Ripley and Marc Lourdes from CNN went to North Korea on a carefully-planned reporting journey, a little broader and more detailed than

Simmons' trip. Ripley and Lourdes relate a story of talking to some North Korean children, who are telling them about their ambitions to join the army "to fight the 'sworn American enemy.'"

> I asked them if they would shoot me if I told them I'm American, and get a quick, unanimous 'yes' in response.

> They then temper their enthusiasm somewhat, saying they'll see if I'm good or bad. I promise I'm a good American. They say they won't shoot me after all.

The article also quotes a young boy who called the current leader, Kim Jong-un, "the father who returns all the love of the real parents." The cult personality that was built around Kim Il-sung back in the days of the war itself has continued to surround his descendants in a positive glow.

Without access to outside perspectives, North Korean children only know what their government tells them about other countries, and what the North Korean government has to say about other countries – *especially* the United States – isn't pretty. The people who were interviewed for CNN matter-of-factly explain that they hate the United States because Americans brutally massacred Koreans during the war, for no real reason. They're not entirely wrong – the Korean war was brutal, and as we will see in the chapter on the United

States, the American military inflicted brutal casualties on Korean civilians. Almost one tenth of North Korean citizens were killed. But while the twentieth century has seen multiple brutal wars – ones with much higher rates of casualties than the Korean war – North Korea has kept the grudge alive in a way that countries like France, Germany, Japan, or even Russia haven't. The continued hatred for the United States shows what happens when a government tells its people that people from another country are evil, and those people have no opportunities to actually interact with that country.

RANDOM FACTS

1. In North Korea, the Korean War is known as the *choguk habang chonjaeng*, or the "Fatherland liberation war."

2. North Korea's official name is the Democratic People's Republic of North Korea. Of course, today, it's not democratic, it's not a republic, and it doesn't serve the needs of its people, so we'll stick with the part of the name that's accurate – just "North Korea."

3. A town in the mountains of North Korea is hailed as Kim Il-sung's birthplace. However, outside scholars think he may have been born in Russia.

4. The North Korean calendar sets the year "0" at the date of Kim Il-sung's birth, rather than the date of Jesus's birth the way the Gregorian calendar does. He was born in 1912, so instead of this year being 2018, the North Korean calendar sets the date at 106.

5. Because Kim Il-sung is the "eternal leader" even though he is dead, this makes North Korea the world's only "necrocracy" – a country governed by the rules of a dead person.

6. North Korea has a law stating that any punishment will last for three generations. So if someone breaks a law, their parents and children (or grandparents

and parents, or children and grandchildren) are all understood to have broken the law, too.

7. The most significant and infamous way of punishing crimes (especially crimes against the state) in North Korea is in prison camps or work camps. Some of these camps are for political prisoners, to stop them from interacting with anyone outside, and some are known as "re-education camps," where prisoners are brainwashed and forced to memorize speeches from North Korean leaders, as well as performing hard labor.

8. Crimes that are worthy of the death penalty in North Korea include watching South Korean media, distributing pornography, and owning a Bible.

9. During a cease-fire in the war, North Korea built a village near the border that has no people. The village is called Kijong-dong, and was designed to look like a prosperous village in order to trick the South Koreans and Americans into believing that North Korea was more economically successful than it was.

10. There is a South Korean town located a similar distance from the border, and these two towns frequently play games of one-upmanship to prove that their country is better. For example, in the 1980s, they competed as to who could build the tallest flagpole, and in the 90s and 2000s, they played louder and louder propaganda messages

through loudspeakers to try to convince people from the other side to join them.

11. In order to maintain the anti-American rhetoric that they developed during the Korean War, the North Korean government has a very tight hold on the country's media. People have TVs, but can only watch three channels that broadcast approved content.

12. People in the twenty-first century North Korea also have smartphones and computers, but can only access an "intranet," where all content is carefully monitored and filtered by the government.

13. Life is so tightly controlled in North Korea that even haircuts have to be approved by Kim Jong-un. There are only 28 approved styles of haircut – ten for men, and eighteen for women.

14. In spite of this tight control, North Korean-ized versions of western forms of media are pretty popular... like the Moranbong Band, the state-approved girl group, for which Kim Jong-un personally chooses members. One of their songs is a cover for the theme from the movie *Rocky*, while other songs praise the North Korean government.

15. The capital of North Korea is Pyongyang. This is a fairly recent development – the former capital of Korea (way before it was split) was a North Korean city called Kaesong. However, it is very close to the

38th parallel, and was the only city to be passed between North and South Korean control during the war.

16. Pyongyang is populated only with the North Korean elite, and therefore projects an unusually positive view of what life is like in North Korea. Any time North Korean media wants to display the country as prosperous and modern, Pyongyang is what they show.

17. Because North Korea severed ties with virtually all its trade partners (except China) after the Korean war, its resources are very limited… so limited that, during a drought, the government demanded that its people provide their own feces to the government for fertilizer.

18. In the period directly following the Korean War, North Korea was on the lookout for potential attacks from the United States… and found them. In 1968, North Korea became the only nation ever to capture and hold an American Navy ship – the USS Pueblo.

19. The first-ever pilot to defect with an active aircraft from North to South Korea was No Kum-sok, on September 21st, 1953.

20. Despite North Korea's small size and lack of resources, it is identified as the greatest threat to world peace and safety today.

Test Yourself – Questions and Answers

1. Who was the Premier of China in 1950?

    a. Mao Zedong
    b. Zhou Enlai
    c. Kim Il-sung

2. What is the correct order (oldest to newest) of North Korean leaders?

    a. Kim Il-sung, Kim Jong-il, Kim Jong-un
    b. Kim Jong-un, Kim Il-sung, Kim Jong-il
    c. Kim Jong-il, Kim Jong-un, Kim Il-sung

3. When did the Stalemate period of the Korean War happen?

    a. 1950-1955
    b. 1951-1953
    c. 1955-present

4. What is *Juche*?

    a. The Soviet ideology of spreading the influence of communism
    b. The South Korean ideology of positive international relationships
    c. The North Korean ideology of self-reliance

5. How does North Korea maintain its dictatorship today?

    a. The government highlights war crimes committed by Americans against Koreans during the Korean War.

b. No contact with media from outside North Korea is allowed, so people have no opportunity to see alternative perspectives.
c. Political dissenters are harshly prosecuted, and they and their families can be sent to prison camps if they speak out against the government.
d. All of the above.

Answers

1. b
2. a
3. b
4. c
5. d

CHAPTER THREE

SOUTH KOREA

So now you know all about what was happening in North Korea – how they got into the war, and also what happened afterwards. But what about South Korea? Today, in 2018, South Korea is a major economic power, with world-famous media, products, and education. But in 1950, it was in just as much of a mess as North Korea was. In this chapter, we're going to learn about what happened in South Korea during the Korean War (and afterwards) that led to it being so much more successful than North Korea is today.

Rhee's Reaction to the Invasion

Let's start with the very first true action of the Korean War: North Korea's invasion of the South on June 25th, 1950. North Korea's stated intention was to execute Rhee Sygnman, the right-wing and pro-American President of South Korea, as a political traitor. Rhee was an authoritarian not quite on the level of Kim Il-sung but definitely above what we might call "democratic," and he knew that if the North Korean army got a hold of him, he wouldn't survive.

On June 27, Rhee Syngman fled from Seoul, the capital of South Korea, knowing that the North Korean army would soon capture it. It was his highest priority that the North Korean army should not capture him – and he wasn't particularly interested in what happened to anyone else. His top priority was to get to safety. But he was also throwing the rest of the city at a bit of a disadvantage, because no one else seemed to believe that North Korea would actually be able to capture the capital city of Seoul. But they did.

The Hangang Bridge

On July 28th, 1950, the South Korean army ordered that the Hangang Bridge over the Han River be blown up. This bridge carried a major highway and was one of the clearest land routes between North and South Korea. They hoped that by destroying this bridge, they would slow or even stop the North Korean invasion.

Unfortunately, the Hangang Bridge was also a means of escape for refugees, and when they blew it up at two in the morning on the 28th, there were four thousand refugees crossing it, hundreds of whom were killed and even more of whom were seriously injured.

Besides that, destroying the bridge trapped South Korean forces, who had been fighting north of the bridge, in enemy territory. With few convenient alternative routes, and questionable means of communication, these military units were practically stranded. It was an extreme measure, and the South Korean army thought for sure that it would show North Korea both that they were serious about the war effort, and that they weren't going to let North Korea into their part of the country, no matter what they had to do to stop them.

Unfortunately for South Korea, the Hangang bridge *didn't* stop them.

The First Battle of Seoul

The first move that the North Korean army made was to attack Seoul. Capturing the South Korean capital would be a massive symbolic victory for them, as well as a tactical one. It would show how serious they were about their attack, and how powerful their army was – destroying any idea that they might be just a weak little upstart local rebel army.

On June 25th, 1950, the North Korean army crossed the 38th parallel and made a beeline for Seoul. They brought the tanks that they had wrestled out of the Soviet Union, and used the blitzkrieg tactics that had become popular in World War II: a front line of armoured vehicles that could break through defensive lines, followed by lightweight and fast-moving attackers that could hit the enemy where they were vulnerable.

South Korea didn't have any weapons that would stand up to a tank invasion. The entire army didn't have one single tank. Besides, they were caught off-guard, under-funded, and under-supplied. With limited resources (some of which the South Korean army kind of trapped in North Korea with the Hangang Bridge incident) and almost no time to prepare, Seoul folded to the North Korean attack in less than three days

The Bodo League Massacre

Rhee Syngman had been spending the last year doing what any good totalitarian leader would do in his situation: he made a plan to get rid of anyone in his country who he thought might sympathize with the enemy. Thus was born Rhee's Bodo League, a "re-education" program for about three hundred thousand suspected communists or communist sympathizers in South Korea. The claim was that these "re-education" programs were an alternative to being imprisoned or executed as political prisoners… but that claim went out the window once the North Korean army attacked. Just two days after the North Korean army crossed the 38th parallel, Rhee ordered mass executions: everyone related to the South Korean Workers Party (the communist party of South Korea), and everyone who had been put into the Bodo League.

There were no trials, and no official sentencing. You

didn't even have to *actually* be a communist, or have any contact with North Korea – being suspected was more than enough. Victims were herded into prisons, or forced to lie on their stomachs before they were shot.

And let's be clear: while there are conflicting accounts of how involved the United States military was in many of the war crimes of the Korean War, this is one that the Americans absolutely did sign off on. American photographers took pictures of the massacre, keeping the gory evidence for the records. One United States lieutenant colonel even told a South Korean colonel that he could kill the political prisoners they were keeping in Busan, if the North Korean army got too close to the city… and, sure enough, three and a half thousand South Koreans were executed in Busan soon after.

The prisoners who were shot were the lucky ones. Other prisoners had their backs broken and were kept alive for days afterwards in the hopes that they would be able to provide some information. If you were unlucky enough to live near the sea, you might be tied up with other prisoners and thrown into the ocean together. This tactic was especially handy, because it got rid of the evidence, and made it just a little bit easier for the government to get away with it.

Balloon Propaganda

As with any war of ideals – a war between two fundamentally different political systems – a huge part of the war effort for both North Korea and South Korea was trying to convince the other side to join their system. Especially given the fact that both North and South Korea were a little short on actual weapons and supplies, trying to sway the other side towards their opinion was the most efficient way to actually make an impact on the war effort.

When travel between North and South Korea was cut off – for instance, because the main bridge connecting them had been bombed – balloon propaganda was the best way to spread influence with the civilians.

What is balloon propaganda? It's what it sounds like – propaganda strapped to a balloon, which is then sent into enemy territory. World War II had been a heyday for balloon propaganda, with thousands of leaflets containing everything from pamphlets of news to unflattering caricatures of leaders dropped all over western Europe. The Korean War expanded the role of balloon propaganda far beyond what it had been in World War II.

Over the course of the war, South Korea printed two and a half *billion* leaflets to drop into North Korea. Besides spreading propaganda, the sheer number of leaflets printed was meant to demonstrate how many more resources South Korea had, compared to North Korea (it's true that they had more, but it was a bit of a weird way to use them, considering how tight they were for weapons and manpower). One famous South

Korean leaflet proclaimed, "Believe Jesus Christ instead of Kim Il-sung," directly attacking the way Kim Il-sung was elevated to the status of a religious figure in North Korea.

Operation Chromite

After the brutal attack and defeat of South Korean forces in the first Battle of Seoul, South Korea had to move fast to get back on track. They didn't have the manpower or the tools that China and the Soviet Union had provided North Korea with, but once it became clear that the invasion had *really* happened (and was really a major attempt by a communist state to invade a non-communist one, i.e. a *big* deal in the Cold War world), they had the United States and the United Nations on their side (for reasons we'll go into more deeply in the next chapter). They could still reverse the damage done by the first North Korean attacks, but they had to move quickly.

Hence, South Korea and the United Nations put their heads together and developed the plan for Operation Chromite, a major amphibious invasion of the North that they planned to use to recapture Seoul and re-establish themselves as the dominant power on the Korean peninsula.

The operation was enormous – think seventy five *thousand* troops (each one containing anywhere from dozens to hundreds of soldiers) and two hundred and sixty one naval vessels. After their inability to gather the resources to fight North Korea's initial attack, South Korea and its allies were eager to demonstrate that they had the tools and resources to hold their own in the war, and that they were not going to lie back and let themselves get trampled the way they had been in the first battle.

The Battle of Incheon

At the moment South Korea was planning to attack, both sides happened to be busy with a major incentive near the Busan port, called the Battle of the Pusan Perimeter. The North Korean army was interested in capturing Busan, which would give them control over the ocean and much better access to resources than they could have otherwise. And it was clear that North Korea was struggling. They were having difficulty transporting food and resources to their soldiers, and they had pretty much only a land army, while their enemies had the United States' air force and navy on their side. North Korea's resources were wearing thin, while South Korea's were only just starting to get moving.

While North Korea was struggling to hold their own near Busan, South Korea made their move on the opposite side of the peninsula. Using their huge amphibious task force, the South Korean and United Nations forces made a move on the city of Incheon, a port town near the border, which North Korea had left mostly undefended while they poured their resources into Busan.

There were almost six times as many United Nations troops as there were North Korean troops in Incheon, and the UN tanks were outfitted with flamethrowers and bulldozer blades to wreak havoc on the city. Between September 10th and September 19th, the South Korean and United Nations forces bombarded the city with air, sea, and land attacks. North Korea didn't have a chance. This was the first decisive victory for South Korea and her allies, and lifted both natural and international spirit. The first couple of months had been bad, but now it looked like maybe South Korea stood a chance.

The Second Battle of Seoul

With control of Incheon, a strategic North Korean position, and one decisive victory under their belts, the South Korean army now turned their attention to recapturing their lost capital. If they had hoped that re-capturing Seoul would be as quick and glorious as capturing Incheon, they were sorely mistaken. Incheon had been virtually undefended, but North Korea was committed to protecting the important and newly-gained city of Seoul.

The North Korean tactic was to forestall the South Korean forces in Incheon and give them time to reinforce their protections around Seoul. They also made a move to withdraw any troops from the south that didn't absolutely need to be there, thus limiting any collateral damage and unnecessary loss of manpower in the inevitable move towards Seoul.

On September 22nd, 1950, the South Korean forces entered Seoul, breaking through the layers of fortifications. Much of the fighting they engaged in was house-to-house fighting, with United States Marines going from door to door and gunning down anyone who looked like they wanted to put up a fight. After three days, Major General Edward Almond, the American commander of the campaign, declared that the battle had been won and Seoul was back in the hands of South Korea.

The Post-Liberation Massacres

After Seoul was officially declared to be back in South Korean hands, the South Korean police force did what it had gotten really good at doing: it rounded up communists and executed them. In two major sets of executions called the Goyang Geumjeong Cave massacre and the Namyangju massacre, people who were suspected of collaborating with the North Korean invaders, or who were suspected of having communist sympathies, or who were *related* to people who were suspected of collaborating with the North Korean invaders or having communist sympathies, were executed without trial. A hundred and fifty people were killed in the Goyang Geumjeong Cave massacre, and four hundred and sixty in the Namyangju massacre. In Goyang, the bodies were buried, and a 2006 Truth and Reconciliation Commission found that they included seven women and eight teenagers.

These massacres were gory, and so severe that the South Korean government has since issued official apologies and started paying reparations to victims, but they were really just an extreme manifestation of the same anti-communist paranoia that was gripping the entire world at the time.

The Battle of Pyongyang

Buoyed by the success at Incheon and the reclaiming of Seoul, the South Korean military moved north, with an eye towards giving North Korea a taste of its own medicine by capturing *their* capital. They wanted to take hold of the city of Pyongyang, and believed that if they could cut off North Korea's capital, they would have truly gained the upper hand in the war.

Just like Rhee Syngman had done when he knew Seoul was about to be captured, Kim Il-sung and his fellow leaders had already made a speedy escape from their capital. They had retreated to Kanggye, a city near the border of China where four major rivers converged. Pyongyang was well-fortified, but had no defenses against the air attack launched by South Korea and the

United States. They cut off the ability of North Korean soldiers to re-enter the city, effectively keeping it under their control.

South Korea managed to hold on to Pyongyang for less than two months. They captured it on October 19th, 1950, but on December 5th of that same year, the Chinese army had rallied forces to repel the American airforce, and North Korea regained control of their capital.

Ha Young Yoon and Life in a Target City

In an interview, a woman named Ha Young Yoon, who was eight years old when the Korean war began, describes what it was like living in a South Korean town that was targeted by North Korean forces. "We were more afraid of the poor people than the *In Meen Goon* [North Korean soldiers]," she remembers. "The poor people led *In Meen Goon* to rich people's houses. Everyone suffered during the war, but the rich people had everything taken away. The rich people became their first target. Actually, *In Meen Goon* were nice. The scarier people were the poor who betrayed us." Ha Young Yoon's house was used as an office by the North Korean soldiers while they were in her city, so she was protected, even though her family was rich.

The focus on taking property from the rich was a feature of the North Korean communist ideology. Although now, in 2018, we've seen that real communist regimes don't tend to serve poor people very well, in the 1950s, there was still a lot of hope among groups of impoverished people that a communist leadership could bring them prosperity. This was probably why the poor people in Ha Young Yoon's town were so eager to help the North Korean invaders, and also why the South Korean police force was so vigilant to the risk of communist sympathizers... the new regime looked pretty attractive.

Negotiations

As we learned in the last chapter, the majority of 1951 through 1953 was a lot of not-very-successful campaigns where one side or the other would make an attack, the other side would rebuff it, and very little territory of strategic importance changed hands. After the first couple of attempts on Seoul and Pyongyang, those cities stayed in their respective countries' capitals for the rest of the war, and into the present.

In 1954, the demilitarized zone was established, and the process of repatriating prisoners of war began, confirming an uneasy peace in Korea. Communication was difficult for both political and practical reasons, but things did eventually settle into a new status quo that involved a swath of military land and a perpetual slight anxiety about the possibility that war might return to ruin more Korean lives.

Unlike North Korea, South Korea rarely, if ever, claims that it won the Korean War. Instead, many South

Korean civilians put it out of their minds entirely and did their best to move back towards their daily lives, enjoying the economic prosperity that globalized economies were finding in the late 1950s and early '60s. And on the other side of the coin, South Korean leaders remained conscious that the war was not really over, and that, at any moment, the wrong move could bring them straight back to 1950.

The South Korean Language

During and after the Korean War, South Korea has become more and more connected to the United States, while North Korea has become more and more isolated. Even though it's only been about seventy years, they have developed distinctly different dialects. South Korea has adopted loan words and phrases from other countries, while North Korea hasn't. For example, both North and South Koreans use cell phones, but in South Korea, they're called "haendeupon" (borrowing the English word *hand*), while in North Korea, they're called "sonjeonwagi" – literally "hand phone." South Korea has moved away from using old-fashioned Chinese vocabulary and towards European words for things that there are no native Korean words for. The North Korean vocabulary also contains many more words describing ideological elements of communism.

Because of this, among North Koreans who have escaped to South Korea, 46% say they have difficulty understanding the language, and 1% say that they can't understand it at all. This is a pretty big difference for only being separated for seventy years!

Armistice Negotiations

Between 1953 and 1954, North and South Korea were locked in a debate about armistice. Both sides had been decimated by the battles of the Stalemate, but neither side wanted to admit defeat… and neither side could envision armistice as anything *except* defeat.

One of the biggest points of argument was how to deal with all the people who had been captured as prisoners of war. Many of the people who had been in the Korean People's Army or the People's Volunteer Army (the North Korean and Chinese armies, respectively) had been captured by the South Korean or American armies, and now refused to go back to North Korea. They said that life was better as a prisoner of war than as a part of their old homes.

The conclusion they eventually came to was that both sides would form a demilitarized zone (DMZ for short) that cut in between North and South Korea… right along the 38th parallel, the line that they had been fighting over the whole time. It was formed on July 27, 1953. There was no peace treaty made or signed, but the sides agreed that no military activity could cross the demilitarized zone, which meant that fighting effectively stopped.

The 1960 Protest against Rhee Syngman

Just because fighting ended with the establishment of the demilitarized zone and the final form of the armistice in 1955, didn't mean that troubles were over for Rhee. On the contrary, he became almost as known for political corruption as his enemies. After the fighting of the Korean War ended, Rhee ordered that politicians who opposed him should be arrested en masse, for suspicion of communist sympathies or other trumped-up charges. Unsurprisingly for someone who had his opponents arrested, he won the election by a landslide – 74%.

But people were not satisfied with Rhee. In March of 1960, the coastal city of Masan erupted in a massive protest against Rhee's corrupt political activities. The thirst for protest spread across South Korea, especially among students – in April, Korea University became the hub of a massive protest against the violence exercised against political dissidents. Only when police started firing into a crowd of students protesting in front of the presidential residence did the crowd disperse, but the pressure was enough to lead Rhee to flee the country. He officially abandoned his post as President on April 26th, 1960, and escaped to America with the CIA's help.

These protests could be said to be part of the same "zeitgeist" and spirit for protest that would later inspire American students to take to the streets with signs to protest their own governmental corruption over the 1960s and 1970s. In some ways, in fact, the American hippies might have been inspired by the Korean protestors, who were brave enough to speak up for justice even in a nation that had just been ravaged by war. If Korean students were brave enough to confront a corrupt leader, the line of thinking went, what excuse could American students have?

RANDOM FACTS

1. General William Lynn Roberts, the commander of the Korean Military Advisory Group, said that an invasion from North Korea would just be "target practice" for the South Korean military.

2. As North Korea's official name is the Democratic People's Republic of North Korea, South Korea's official name is simply the Republic of Korea.

3. Balloon propaganda campaigns are still popular in Korea today. Recent campaigns have involved dropping instant noodles, friendly letters to North Korean civilians, USB sticks with pages from Korean Wikipedia, and copies of the movie *The Interview*, a humorous film about a plan to assassinate Kim Jong-un.

4. General Douglass MacArthur, who commanded the American forces at the Battle of Incheon, is commemorated in a massive statue at Jayu Park in present-day Incheon. The park also features a monument commemorating the friendship between Korea and the United States.

5. The North Koreans had determined that a landing on the Incheon channel would be impossible, which was the reason they were caught so off-

guard by the South Korean army's use of an amphibious attack on Incheon.

6. One of the key elements to the Incheon attack was the element of surprise... which South Korea found severely compromised. The Japanese press had gotten wind of the planned attack, and was mysteriously referring to it in the media as "Operation Common Knowledge." Fortunately for South Korea, the Japanese "common knowledge" didn't reach North Korea.

7. Douglas MacArthur had promised the South Korean government that he would get their capital back, and felt it was his personal mission to uphold that promise.

8. Edward Almond, the Major General in charge of the Second Battle of Seoul, was eager to claim that the city was liberated, and sent out the message saying it had been conquered on September 25th, even though soldiers were still fighting in the streets.

9. Rhee is name-dropped in Billy Joel's hit song "We Didn't Start the Fire," which is a catalogue of major political events in the second half of the twentieth century. The first verse ends with references to "North Korea, South Korea, Marilyn Monroe," but later in the song, Syngman Rhee appears by name in the line "U2, Syngman Rhee, payola and Kennedy."

10. Rhee spent the last few years of his life in Honolulu, where he died in 1965.

11. One of the reasons that North Korea posed such a genuine threat to South Korea during the Korean War was that there were so many seriously impoverished people in South Korea to whom communism looked like not only a viable, but a *great* alternative. Since then, South Korea has worked to reduce poverty in its resource-poor territories by becoming a "knowledge economy," where a strictly meritocratic school system tries to balance out economic disparity. There are many issues with South Korea's school system, but it does seem to be doing its job – South Korea has the eleventh-highest GDP in the world, despite being small and lacking in natural resources.

12. The biggest modern challenge to South Korea's economic success is the continued and constant threat of war breaking out again.

13. South Koreans born after 1955 are, on average, two inches taller than North Koreans born in the same period, probably due to better access to resources and food.

14. South Korea provided prostitutes for its soldiers. These women were expected to be *extremely* efficient, having sex with at least twenty nine men every day, and never for longer than half an hour

with any one man.

15. American troops are still stationed in South Korea in case North Korea attempts to invade again.

16. In South Korea, the Korean War is sometimes known as "625" or "the 6-2-5 Upheaval" because North Korea invaded on June 25th, or 6/25.

17. South Korea had an active secret police that worked during and after the war to root out sympathizers. If they hadn't been up against such an obvious totalitarian state, they probably would have faced a lot more criticism for this.

18. One of the most common injuries among foot soldiers during the Korean War was actually frostbite. Korea can get very cold, especially in its northern and mountainous regions, and the troops were not adequately prepared for the weather.

19. Discussions about the truce between North and South Korea lasted for two years and seventeen days in total before a truce was declared.

20. South Korea suffered slightly less military deaths than North Korea: About 217,000 compared to 406,000. However, their civilian death rates were much higher – North Korea lost about six hundred thousand civilians, while over a million South Koreans were declared dead or missing during the conflict.

Test Yourself – Questions and Answers

1. What is the Korean War called in South Korea?

    a. The Fatherland Liberation War
    b. The Civil War
    c. The 6-2-5 Upheaval

2. Where did Rhee Syngman die?

    a. Honolulu
    b. San Francisco
    c. Miami

3. What makes the South Korean language different from the North Korean language?

    a. South Korea has adopted more loanwords from English and other European languages
    b. North Korea uses more traditional Chinese vocabulary
    c. The North Korean language includes many more words describing communism and communist ideas
    d. All of the above

4. What does DMZ stand for?

    a. Deadly Mechanical Zephyrs
    b. Drop, March, Zigzag
    c. Demilitarized Zone

5. What was the name for the amphibious attack on North Korea?

    a. Operation Crocodile
    b. Operation Chromite
    c. Operation Chamomile

Answers

1. c
2. a
3. d
4. c
5. b

CHAPTER FOUR

THE UNITED STATES AND THE UNITED NATIONS IN KOREA

Just five years after the end of World War II, American soldiers were not excited to enlist in the army to fight in Korea. But the government's interests trumped the interests of the individuals – and from the American government's perspective, nothing could be more important than fighting a war that would prevent communism from spreading into another country.

"A Defensive Measure"

The CIA almost immediately noticed that the North Korean army was moving south – but they weren't particularly worried. An official report from the CIA stated that they thought this movement was "a defensive measure" and that war was "unlikely." They kept an eye on the movements of North Korea, but didn't believe for a moment (as far as anyone knew) that North Korea was actually serious about a threat of war against South Korea or the American forces stationed there.

Recently declassified CIA documents show that the United States was completely unprepared for a genuine threat of war, and was blindsided when North Korea invaded. A January memorandum says that the movement of the North Korean army towards the border was probably "a defensive measure to offset the growing strength of the offensively minded South Korean army."

It was because of their lack of preparedness that they scrambled to gather resources to counter the attack, and by the time they did, North Korean forces had gained control of much of the Korean peninsula.

The Home-by-Christmas Offensive

Starting in October, 1950, the American government branded the Korean War effort as a war that would not last long. People were unwilling to go to war again just five years after the end of World War II, especially to fight in what many Americans perceived as a geopolitically insignificant country.

General Douglas MacArthur, who had risen to prominence in the pacific theatre of World War II, assured President Harry Truman that they had no reason to fear Chinese intervention, and that without

Chinese help, the North Koreans would fold within months. They just didn't have the resources to sustain a long-term offensive. MacArthur assured Truman, who in turn, assured the American people, that any soldiers who joined the Korean War would be "home by Christmas."

Just as a reminder, the last time before this that a country told its people that they would be "home by Christmas" after going to war was in World War I, and we all know how *that* turned out.

As it turned out, MacArthur was one hundred percent wrong about Chinese intervention. The Chinese army *did* intervene in Korea, which prompted MacArthur to admit his mistake to the American government by telling them, "We face an entirely new war."

The United Nations in Korea

The United States might have been most invested in the Korean War – both because they had been in charge of the invaded South Korea, and because they were the nation that was most worried about the spread of communism – but they weren't the only country that made a quick and intense commitment to the Korean War effort on behalf of South Korea. Twenty-one member nations of the United Nations committed to assisting South Korea. Australia, Great Britain, Canada, France, Belgium, the Netherlands, Colombia, Ethiopia, South Africa, New Zealand, Turkey, Greece, Thailand, the Philippines, and Luxembourg all sent units to fight in the war (as well as the United States, of course). Norway, Sweden, Denmark, India, and Italy did not send fighting forces, but did contribute medical support, including military hospitals, trained doctors, and field ambulances.

With all of this support, it might be hard to imagine how there was even a competition. But remember, these countries had basically all either just been decimated by World War II, or just come out under the thumb of colonial rule. So while they were quite the lineup, their support was more useful for showing support than for actually providing supplies or manpower. Not that they weren't useful – just not as useful as that long list might have you believe.

Staff Sergeant Reckless

One of the most famous war heroes of the Korean War wasn't the typical tactical genius or skilled hand-to-hand combatant who rises to fame in war efforts... It was a war horse.

A Mongolian mare, bred for racing, Sergeant Reckless was bought from a racetrack in Seoul and trained to be a pack animal for the United States Marine Corps. She carried ammunition in the battlefields, helped wounded soldiers escaped to safety, and, in March 1953, famously made more than fifty re-supply trips to the front lines of the Battle for Outpost Vegas. She was famous for not needing human handlers to guide her, but instead being able to reach areas that most humans didn't dare go to.

She was also a great asset to the United States army because, unlike normal soldiers, she wasn't a picky eater… she ate scrambled eggs, beer, Coca-Cola, and, on one occasion, the camp's entire supply of poker chips. She has been decorated with a Purple Heart, a Korean Service Medal, and a Navy Presidential Unit Citation, among other awards and medals.

Kurt Lee

Major Kurt Chew-Een Lee was the first officer of the United States Marine Corps of Chinese decent. He was involved in the United States Marine Corps during World War II, and had been recruited to learn and teach Japanese, but hadn't gotten to see any real action during the war, much to his disappointment. During the Korean War, he finally got his chance to shine.

Lee said that he wanted to set a good example for Chinese-Americans in the military, and "wanted to dispel the notion about the Chinese being weak, meek, and obsequious." He was the kind of guy who dreamed of a big, honourable, and glorious death in battle, and said that he didn't expect to survive the Korean War, but wanted his death to "be spectacular."

Kurt rose up quickly through the ranks for his bravery

and dedication, but besides being a brave soldier, he was also *great* at confusing the enemy. He commanded his platoon in Mandarin Chinese, baffling the enemy Chinese troops, and catching them off-guard before making his attacks.

Benjamin Wilson

Benjamin Wilson was an American soldier who had missed out on active duty in World War II, and was eager to see some real combat in Korea. So eager, in fact, that even being carried away on a medical stretcher wouldn't stop him from fighting.

He was given the job of leading the charge against North Korea on the Hwachon Reservoir, in a battle so deadly that the Reservoir would later be nicknamed "Hell Hill." Wilson enthusiastically moved his company up the hill, despite the enemy fire that was raining down on them. He stormed a machine gun bunker and killed all the men in it, then went on to fight hand-to-hand, using bayonets and fists to fight off the Chinese soldiers defending the hill. Then he charged the force, *alone*, and killed seven men, wounded two, and dispersed the entire rest of the fleet, even though he was only one man.

Even after that, it looked like Wilson wouldn't be enough to overrun the forces. He was seriously injured, and put onto a stretcher to be carried down the hill. But when the medics set the stretcher down, Wilson, not to be deterred, got up off of it – in spite of his injuries – and climbed the hill again to join his men.

The Battle of the Chosin Reservoir

The Battle of the Chosin Reservoir, which was fought between American and Chinese forces from November 17th to December 13th, 1950, was one of the single deadliest offensives in the entire Korean War – but it wasn't just soldiers who were responsible for the huge death count. Mother Nature had a role to play, too.

Temperatures dropped as low as -47 degrees Celsius (-54 degrees Fahrenheit) – colder than the North Pole at the same time of year. 1,029 American soldiers were killed in battle… and 7,338 were killed by something other than the battle, mostly frostbite. On the Chinese side, 19,202 soldiers were killed in battle, and 28,954 were killed by frostbite and other factors.

Although the United States withdrew their troops from the Chosin Reservoir, which gave the Chinese total control over North Korea, the costs of battle to the Chinese army were so great that the victory was hardly worth it. Forty percent of the Chinese forces had been damaged by the battle, and didn't recover until the following spring.

An American soldier who had been involved in the Battle of the Chosin Reservoir later designed a bumper sticker that read "Hell froze over. We were there."

Bayonets

The twentieth century saw major developments in military technology, and the Korean War was a testing ground for many of them. But one classic American standby weapon also had its time to shine: the bayonet. Bayonets were long, triangular spears that were attached to rifles, so that soldiers could engage in hand-to-hand combat without having to carry a separate sword. They were used during the Revolutionary War, the War of 1812, and the American Civil War, but by the Korean War, you might think that they would have gone out of style. Not so.

The last major American bayonet charge was led on February 7th, 1951, by Officer Lewis Millett, and earned him the Medal of Honor . Millett attacked Hill 180 with bayonets and hand grenades, and although he was seriously wounded by shrapnel, he refused to evacuate the hill until after the position was secured for American forces.

S. L. A. Marshall, a war historian, described it as "the most complete bayonet charge by American troops since Cold Harbor" (a battle during the American Civil War).

"A Bit Sticky"

In 1951, the Gloucestershire Regiment, a regiment of 600 British soldiers faced off to 30,000 Chinese soldiers at the Imjin River. The British troop was vastly outnumbered and had no hope of success. Tom Brodie, the Brigadier of the regiment, contacted his American superior to describe the situation and ask for backup.

"It's a bit sticky," he said.

He was using a classic British understatement, but the American supervisor, not understanding Brodie, assumed that if it was only "a bit sticky," the regiment could handle it. He didn't send reinforcements or give permission to retreat.

The Gloucestershire Regiment fought impressively, and ten thousand Chinese troops fell during the battle, but while less than a hundred of the British soldiers were killed, all but thirty-nine were captured.

Turkey in the Korean War

The United States was the main force siding with South Korea in the Korean War, backed up by multiple other members of the United Nations who were dedicated to preventing the spread of communism. The countries that were involved, like Britain and Canada, were often very attached to the United States, politically and economically – although this wasn't the case for every single ally, more of them than not were very America-ish.

This wasn't the case for Turkey. Turkey had no political affiliation towards either the American or the

Soviet side of the Cold War, and thus would have had every reason to stay out of the Korean War. However, they were interested in gaining American favor so that they could become part of NATO, which they had previously been denied entry for. To curry that favor, they sent soldiers to aid the American troops in the Korean War.

There were some challenges – like the fact that the Brigadier General who was in charge of commanding the Turkish forces didn't speak any English, which was a bit of a challenge working with the Americans (you can bet that most of them didn't speak any Turkish). But they did curry that favor – Douglas MacArthur said of their forces:

> The military situation in Korea is being followed with concern by the whole American public. But in these concerned days, the heroism shown by the Turks has given hope to the American nation. It has inculcated them with courage... the American public understands that the United Nations Forces in Korea were saved from encirclement and from falling into the hands of the communists by the heroism shown by the Turks.

Lieutenant John Thorton and Life in a POW Camp

Both sides of the Korean War placed enemy soldiers and internal dissidents alike in Prisoner-of-War camps.

Some of these camps were comparatively innocuous (as much as any place that a person is *forced* to stay can be innocuous), while others were on the level of the concentration camps of World War II. But all the camps shared one thing: everyone there was slowly going crazy from isolation and boredom.

Lieutenant John Thorton, for example, amused himself with his imaginary motorcycle. His story is documented in the book *Voices from the Korean War* by Richard Peters and Xiaobing Li.

Every morning, Thorton would show up to roll call riding his "motorcycle." "With unmistakable sound effects, John would circle the group several times, park his motorcycle, and join the formation." It was only what every cool guy of the 1950s would do. But the men running the camp didn't exactly think that Thorton's motorcycle fit with his position as, you know, their prisoner.

"They called John to their headquarters and informed him that he could no longer keep his motorcycle, because it was against camp 'rules and regulations'," say Peters and Xiaobing. Thorton left the office, dejected at having his property "confiscated." Remarkably, when he told his fellow prisoners about what had happened, they banded together and demanded that the camp leaders "give it back."

Napalm

Napalm was one of the great military innovations of the twentieth century. It was invented in 1942, when scientists accidentally created it while looking for a synthetic alternative to rubber. They found that they could make a powder that wasn't sticky when it was dry, but that could be combined with gasoline to create what amounted to flammable glue. Although it became much more famous for its use in Vietnam, the Korean War was a testing ground for this gory new weapon.

Napalm is made of two main ingredients: a flammable liquid, like gasoline, plus the gelling agent (the powder that the scientists developed), which will make the liquid thick and sticky. The gelling agent will cause the liquid to adhere to pretty much anything it touches – trees, crops, buildings, tanks, and, most horrifyingly, human skin. Once it's on, you can't get it off – at least, not quickly or easily. The developers also added phosphorous, which helped it penetrate through human flesh, so that the burning substance would be especially dangerous and painful for humans. It could penetrate deep into skin and muscle and drive the burning liquid deeper. Besides that, when it burns, napalm lets off large amounts of carbon monoxide and carbon dioxide, so if the victim (or the people around the victim) didn't die of immolation first, they would be suffocated by the smoke. It became the United States' perfect weapon.

Napalm was so effective that the United States army didn't even need to spray it to get the desired effect. Just flying napalm planes overhead had North Korean forces surrendering rather than risk getting sprayed.

Bill Speakman and his Beer Bottles

Not every attack in the Korean War used state-of-the-art weapons like napalm... one British soldier, Bill Speakman, got a little more rustic with his weapons.

On November 4th, 1951, Speakman's Unit (the King's Own Scottish Borderers) was attacked by Chinese soldiers. They were using a tried-and-true technique: start off with a heavy barrage of artillery, force the enemy to waste all their ammunition trying to hold that off, and then push through with a "human wave" of foot soldiers. It was late in the artillery part of this tactic that Speakman decided he needed to take action. He was only a private at the time, and had not received any orders to do anything out of the ordinary, but he couldn't just stand by.

He grabbed six other men and an armful of grenades, and started hurling them willy-nilly at the enemy. The grenades bounced on the frozen ground and did some serious damage to the attack, but there just weren't enough of them. Speakman and his friends were holding them off, but they would quickly be out of ammunition.

Grenades were scarce, but do you know what the camp had a lot of? Empty beer bottles. When you're in a war, you make do with what you have.

When Speakman ran out of grenades, he turned to beer bottles without missing a beat, throwing them at the enemy with all his strength. While they couldn't exactly beat a grenade, the sheer force, broken glass, and surprise at the tactics did forestall the attackers, and gave the rest of the unit time to adopt a better position to handle the "human wave" attack. Speakman was awarded the Victoria Cross, the highest honor a British soldier can receive, for his tactic in this battle.

Operation Paul Bunyan

One of the most famous was actually carried out more than twenty years after the bulk of the fighting was over… and with nothing but axes.

The year was 1976, and the Cold War was still raging. The DMZ was a hotbed of political stress, with both North and South Korea constantly accusing each other of sending spies into each other's territories. To try to control the alleged spying, and the not-alleged, actually-happened tunneling that North Korea was doing, the United Nations set up command posts to keep an eye on both sides of the conflict. One of these command posts, Command Post #3, was particularly near North Korean territory... and ran some risks because of that. Specifically, North Korea kept trying to kidnap the UN soldiers stationed there.

The soldiers at the other command posts tried to keep a close eye on Command Post #3, but that wasn't an easy task, because it was right in the middle of a cluster of trees... and in the summer, when there was a lot of foliage, one *particular* poplar tree was *right* in the line of sight between Command Post #3 and the nearest observation post.

On August 18th, the UN sent five South Korean soldiers, and an American escort of twelve troops, to chop down the poplar.

Now's a good time to mention one of the rules of the DMZ – no weapons. The whole reason it's *demilitarized* is that no one in it is allowed to carry any firearms, explosives, or similar weapons of war. So the soldiers entering didn't bring in any of their weapons. Just axes to cut the poplar down.

They had barely gotten started on the tree when North Korean soldiers arrived on the spot. They demanded that they stop. They insisted that the poplar tree had been planted by Kim Il-sung, and that chopping it down would be an affront to his name (remember the cult of personality we talked about before?). The North Korean soldiers threatened death if the South Korean soldiers didn't comply.

Can you blame the would-be lumberjacks for fleeing? They dropped their axes and tried to make an escape, but, undeterred, the North Korean forces picked up the axes and attacked. They killed the American commanding officer and one other American soldier, and injured all five South Korean soldiers.

The Neutral Nations Repatriation Commission

The armistice saw a massive conflict over the issue of repatriation. The United Nations and United States supported voluntarily repatriation – in other words, people could choose whether and when they wanted to go back to their "home country." They assumed, probably correctly, that most American/South Korean prisoners of war would probably want to leave North Korea and go back to a democratic nation that wasn't a war zone. North Korea and China, on the other hand, supported mandatory repatriation – in other words, people would have to go back to their "home country" when the capturing country told them to. They assumed, probably equally correctly, that most Chinese/North Korean prisoners of war would probably not want to leave South Korea or the United States and go back to a totalitarian dictatorship. The inability to reach a decision on this issue held up armistice for *months*.

The Neutral Nations Repatriation Commission was a

board made up of countries that hadn't been involved in the war. The United Nations chose Sweden and Switzerland as neutral but capitalist-friendly countries, and China chose Poland and Czechoslovakia as neutral but communist-friendly countries. To break the tie, they brought in India, which had supported both sides with medical assistance during the war, and was *well* outside the Cold War power play.

They came to the decision that prisoners of war could refuse to re-enter their home country, and could be kept in NNRC care for up to 120 days while their case was reviewed and arrangements were made. This satisfied both sides, and in February of 1953, most prisoners of war were successfully repatriated.

RANDOM FACTS

1. The Korean War was the first real face-to-face conflict the United States engaged in after World War II.

2. More bombs were dropped by the United States in Korea during the Korean war than by the United States and Japan combined in World War II.

3. The United States resisted dropping an atom bomb on Korea, however, because they suspected that they might be seen as both racist and unnecessarily aggressive if they dropped an atom bomb on *another* small Asian country.

4. A major concern of the United States was that, if North Korea established communist government across the entire Korean peninsula, its next move would be to establish communist government in Japan, which the United States was trying to remake in its own image after World War II.

5. The United States military sometimes used the phrase "tootsie rolls" (the name of a brown gummy candy) as a code word for mortar rounds. This caused confusion when they accidentally ordered hundreds of crates of candy.

6. Four American soldiers defected to North Korea

during the course of the war. They believed that life under North Korea would be better than life back in America.

7. Twenty-one American soldiers defected to China immediately after the war. However, most of them returned to America after some time.

8. The last UN prisoners of war were only released from captivity in China in August 1955, two and a half years after the Neutral Nations Repatriation Commission determined the conditions for repatriation and most prisoners of war were returned.

9. Hostilities ended on July 27th, 1953. However, in the United States, it is considered that the Korean War lasted until the end of January, 1955. This is because the peace after 1953 was so tenuous that Congress wanted to extend the possibility of benefits for more of its soldiers, so they did not declare the war over until 1955.

10. The American president, Harry Truman, never actually asked Congress for a declaration of war in the first place. This means that, officially, from an American point of view, the Korean War is a "police action," not a war.

11. Of the approximately 54,200 American deaths in the Korean war, only about 33,700 were killed in battle. Others died of illness or injury. Frostbite

was the biggest killer.

12. About one quarter of Americans were killed during the Korean War between August 1950, and December 1950. The Battle of Chosin Reservoir was one of the biggest killers, along with the Battle of the Pusan Perimeter, and the Battle of Kuni-ri Pass.

13. One and a half thousand American dogs served in the Korean War.

14. Clint Eastwood, the movie star, was drafted to go into the Korean War. He was stunned that another draft was active so soon after the Second World War had ended. "Wait a second," he famously said. "Didn't we just get through with that?"

15. On September 8th, 1950, the Korean War saw the first air battle carried out using only jet airplanes.

16. The Korean War revolutionized the use of MASH units – Mobile Army Surgical Hospitals. These mobile hospitals could be closer to battle areas than traditional hospitals, and saved thousands of lives. They were also immortalized in the television show M*A*S*H in the 1970s, which is one of the most significant television shows set during the Korean War.

17. For a brief time, President Truman planned to liberate North Korea from its communist rule, as

well as, defending South Korea. However, with China's intervention, it quickly became clear that that wouldn't be possible, and Truman went back to his original plan of just defending South Korea

18. In 1991, both North and South Korea were admitted into the United Nations.

19. The United States awarded 131 Medals of Honor during the Korean War.

20. From an American perspective, the Korean War has been vastly overshadowed by the Vietnam War, which started in the same period but dragged into the 1970s and cost many more American lives.

Test Yourself – Questions and Answers

1. When was the Battle of the Chosin Reservoir?

   a. November 27-December 13, 1950
   b. December 24-December 26, 1951
   c. January 3-February 28, 1952

2. What kind of tree was the focus of Operation Paul Bunyan?

   a. Spruce
   b. Oak
   c. Poplar

3. What was confiscated from Lieutenant John Thorton at the Prisoner of War camp?

   a. His cigarettes
   b. His buttons
   c. His imaginary motorcycle

4. Which leader described being vastly outnumbered and overpowered as "a bit sticky"?

   a. Benjamin Wilson
   b. Tom Brodie
   c. Douglas MacArthur

5. Which country was admitted into the United Nations first?

   a. North Korea
   b. South Korea
   c. They were admitted at the same time

Answers

1. a
2. c
3. c
4. b
5. c

CHAPTER FIVE

CHINA AND THE SOVIET UNION IN KOREA

So now we know what was going on with the capitalist side of the Korean War. But what about the other allies? China and the Soviet Union had their own reasons and their own narratives surrounding the Korean War. In this chapter, we're going to learn what was going on with them, and why they agreed to put so much effort into a tiny, resource-poor country that they could have easily let fall to the United States.

The Zero Sum Game

As we know from Chapter One, the Korean War was a facet of the Cold War, which was the long period of conflict between capitalist nations and communist nations. The Korean War was the first active outbreak of hostilities, the first time these nations actually aligned with fighting territories and created a proxy war. But the context of the Korean War as part of the

Cold War was also a little different than, say, the Vietnam War a few years later.

When the Korean War began, the Cold War was not yet the massive battle of personalities between the United States and Soviet Union that it would become a couple of years down the line. There was not yet an "iron curtain" that divided "east from west" and suggested that communists were living in a totally different world than capitalists.

In fact, the Korean War was the first time that the struggle between communism and capitalism, and especially between the forces of the Soviet Union and the United States, was framed as a zero-sum game that was going to have a winner and a loser. It was the first time that either side (mostly the United States, but both sides did play this) indicated that they thought a world with both communist and capitalist states simply couldn't exist. As the war escalated, both sides developed intense anxiety about what would happen if the other side won this first, flagship victory. If Korea became a communist state, would it signal that a total communist world order was just a few years away? If it became a capitalist state, would it mark the beginning of the end for communism?

Communist Expansionism

The American notion of communist expansionism became vastly overblown during the 1950s and 1960s, developing into full-on nationalist paranoia. American political commenters believed (and told the American public to believe) that it was the sole goal of communist countries to spread their political doctrine to as many non-communist countries as they could, so that eventually the communists (and, let's be real, specifically Joseph Stalin) could rule the world with their evil economic doctrine.

The United States got pretty ridiculous about it, but the idea didn't come from nowhere. Communist countries were definitely *very* interested in spreading their political philosophy to other nations, and Korea seemed like the perfect candidate. For one thing, it bordered on both China and the Soviet Union. This meant that it should, in theory, be pretty easy to take control of – and there were real stakes they didn't, because having an American military holding *right next to* the two most significant communist powers didn't seem like a great idea. So Korea could act as either a gateway to more communist expansion, or simply as a buffer between an aggressive capitalist space (South Korea) and a communist power centre (Chinese Manchuria).

Besides that, Korea didn't have a long history of independent government that they had to overturn, and it was suffering from economic instability and rampant poverty thanks to imperial efforts from Japan and other nations. The fact that it was small and resource-poor made civilians more likely to be drawn to more extreme economic plans that promised to have answers for what they had been told were unsolvable problems. In short, Korea looked like the perfect place for communism to get a nice little toehold before the communist nations made a play for bigger, more powerful, and more resource-rich countries.

Fear of American Influence

China had another specific reason for intervening in Korea, besides simply being interested in the genuine communist expansion plan. They were facing a very real and reasonable concern that the United States might try to invade China. After all, the United States was at *least* as visible and aggressively expansionist as any communist nation, and had the resources to back it up. The Chinese Communist party needed to show that they were willing and able to fight in a serious not-just-civil war on behalf of communism, as well as establish a communist buffer zone around them.

The presence of American military fighting so close to home was also limiting the Chinese forces' ability to respond to internal anti-communist threats. They were (probably rightly) concerned that the presence of American forces would stir up more anti-communist sentiment in the northernmost parts of Korea, and in the Chinese territories adjacent to them. With that risk, it was hard for the new communist regime in China to establish its own credibility – it felt like they were always cowering.

The Forces Meant for Taiwan

They might have had good reasons to want to get involved in North Korea, but one of the reasons that China was hesitant to put too many resources into North Korea's expansionist plan was that they didn't really have that many resources that they could allocate to the project to begin with. After all, they had just finished having a major civil war, installed new communist leadership (traditionally a resource-intensive process), and were not exactly the economic powerhouse they are now. Plus, they had their eye on another small Asian country… Taiwan.

In June, 1950, right around the time that North Korea was planning its attack on the South, China launched an invasion against Taiwan. They had claimed the territory in 1945, but were debating with Japan over who had the rights to it (the native Taiwanese certainly didn't). In 1950, they made an attack that they hoped would definitively put it in their hands, but they were blocked by a United States fleet that was concerned about Taiwan becoming communist Chinese territory. China had to withdraw its attack against Taiwan, but they still had all those military resources… Mao Zedong made the decision to reroute the resources meant for invading Taiwan towards aiding North

Korea in gaining control over the Korean peninsula instead. So, you could say that North Korea exists for the same reason Taiwan does today.

The Chinese People's Volunteer Army

The Chinese army was known as the Chinese People's Volunteer Army, or PVA for short, but make no mistake, these weren't untrained civilians "volunteering" for military service. The army had been trained by decades of intense fighting. All the units of the Chinese People's Volunteer Army had previously been part of the People's Liberation Army.

The People's Liberation Army had its roots in guerrilla warfare that had been fought in China for the past half-century. They had just come out of the Chinese Civil War, which was an extended war that weeded out all but the best. Prior to that, the Chinese People's Volunteer Army had stood up to the Japanese military before and during World War II – a much more strategically organized *and* ambitious army project.

The Chinese People's Volunteer Army was distinctive for its egalitarian uniform style, and its relatively minimal weaponry. All members of the Chinese People's Volunteer Army, no matter how high or low-ranking they were, wore a cotton or wool shirt and trousers in green and khaki colors. The leaders' uniforms were decorated with red piping and tabs on the collars, but they were fairly similar to their subordinates', and all uniforms were designed with warmth and practicality foremost in mind. Their weaponry was simple, but that might have said more about the resources that China had to send to Korea, rather than any specific ideology about how an army should be run.

The Element of Surprise

China made several moves that were meant to prevent the United States from getting a really accurate feel for the scope of their planned attack. For one thing, they did not officially declare war. The fact that they called their army in Korea the "People's Volunteer Army" (even though it was made up entirely of trained forces) was also important, because it allowed China to claim no responsibility for their actions.

These decisions were made so that China could launch an efficient surprise attack rather than being weighed down by boring little things like diplomatic process. They also hoped that a surprise attack would be more effective at ending fighting quickly, with as little damage to their forces as possible. If they fought on equal terms and even ground, Mao Zedong knew that his army was objectively far less well-equipped than the American one, and they wouldn't have much of a chance.

The Soviet Element

The Chinese People's Volunteer Army was certainly important to the war effort in North Korea, but if it had just been China and North Korea versus the United States and South Korea, China and North Korea wouldn't have stood a chance. Chinese forces were well-trained and posed a huge threat in comparison to just the North Korean forces, but they were also radically undersupplied and, as we just learned, were relying almost totally on the element of surprise to gain an advantage. The thing about the element of surprise is that it really only works once.

So there was the Soviet Union. The coalition between the Soviet Union and China in support of North Korea is a complex political topic, which has been the subject of serious academic study but not much popular understanding.

Zhang Xiaoming, in an article for the Journal of Conflict Studies, has argued that the Soviet Union provided equipment, advice and experience, and martial support, especially in the form of air warfare, but that "Soviet Premier Joseph Stalin's fear of a direct confrontation with the United States limited Soviet involvement and assistance in Korea."

In short, the Soviet Union had a lot to lose if they put all their forces into the Korean War. While it would certainly be simplistic to say that China and North Korea were naïve for thinking they could face off with the United States (also, inaccurate, since they did manage it), the Soviet Union was much more conscious of how powerful the United States was in comparison to them, which put a serious damper on their desire to get personally involved. But in spite of that damper, get personally involved they did, and the Soviet Union's material and nominal support for North Korea became one of the leading reasons they were able to fight and take action so successfully.

Did Russia Approve the Attack on South Korea?

Historians continue to clash about whether Stalin actually *knew* that Kim Il-sung was planning an attack on South Korea, or if he simply gave his tacit support *if* a conflict ever happened. The historian Adam Ulam called it "inconceivable" that North Korea could have moved without Soviet support, but Joyce and Gabriel Kolko think that North Korea might have moved on its own. Robert Simmons takes a middle ground, saying that the Soviet Union probably anticipated and supported the invasion, but that North Korea jumped the gun and invaded sooner than the Soviet Union had anticipated, catching them off-guard.

To some extent, any scholar's understanding of the Soviet Union's knowledge about the North Korean attack is going to reflect how powerful they think the Soviet Union was. If you assume that the Soviet Union was a kind of all-powerful, all-seeing totalitarian state that had power over all foreign communist nations (a popular and not baseless reading of Soviet influence), then yes, it makes sense to assume that they were fully aware of and in support of the attack. On the other hand, if you understand the Soviet Union as merely the *most powerful* communist state, but as one that only had control over other communist states insofar as other states were likely to pursue Soviet support because the Soviet Union had the most resources, then they probably didn't specifically sign off on the North Korean attack.

Much like China with their "People's Volunteer Army," the Soviet Union put up barriers against being accused of actually helping North Korea. They insisted that they were not involved or providing military aid, even when they clearly were.

The Soviet Union versus the United Nations

The Soviet Union happened to be one of the most powerful nations in the United Nations, and was very obstinately getting in the way of the UN's efforts to intervene in Korea – yet another way that the Soviet Union was pushing their agenda without *technically* declaring war. They had veto power in the UN, and could have just vetoed every war-related motion that the UN tried to pass, except that they had spent the six months before the Korean War started boycotting every UN meeting. They were boycotting because they didn't like that the Taiwanese (and capitalist) Republic of China had a permanent seat on the UN Security

Council, and the mainland (communist) People's Republic of China didn't.

Boycotting aside, the Soviet Union made many arguments against the legitimacy of the war. For one thing, Korea was not part of the United Nations, and North Korea had not even been invited to be a temporary member. Besides that, the fighting was a civil war, which the UN did not have precedent to intervene in. However, despite the Soviet Union's protests, the UN Security Council publically and unanimously condemned North Korea's invasion of South Korea, and, as we have seen, didn't take the Soviet Union's concerns nearly seriously enough to actually not become involved in the war effort.

General Nam Il

General Nam Il, born in Far East Russia to Korean parents, had flawless communist credentials. He was educated at the Smolensk Military School, and had served in the Soviet Army during the Second World War, where he participated in the Battle of Stalingrad, one of the Soviet Union's greatest and most iconic victories. After World War II ended, Nam moved to Korea.

With that rock-solid background, he became the Chief of Staff for the North Korean People's Army, and when it came time to negotiate and sign the armistice, this Soviet-trained soldier was the man that North Korea chose for the job. He negotiated on behalf of both the Korean People's Army and the Chinese People's Volunteer Army – and, implicitly, on behalf of the Soviet Union's interests – and was hailed far and wide as a genius negotiator.

At least one writer, Christoph Bluth, has suggested that Nam was executed because the powers in North Korea were worried that he was getting too powerful and popular, and might become a rival to Kim Il-sung in the public imagination.

Soviet Archives

The majority of our present knowledge about Soviet involvement in the Korean War actually comes from a set of secret archives that were opened in the 1990s, after the Soviet Union dissolved. These archives contained the previously classified details of the Soviet Union's involvement and plans for supporting North Korea throughout the war. Prior to this, while the Soviet Union had admitted that they were supporting North Korea, no one had known *how* exactly they were supporting them, or to what extent.

It's especially interesting that this information stayed locked up in archives because, in a way, North Korea was the Soviet Union's only actual success when it came to spreading communism and the Soviet sphere of influence. Efforts to expand communism in Europe had generally been rebuffed at best, and resulted in serious foreign policy problems at worst. The Soviet Union had no success spreading communist ideology to the west, moderate success holding on to their possessions in eastern Europe, and increasing internal strife. North Korea, which became a communist power without the Soviet Union conquering it, and *remained* one after the USSR was dissolved, could have been communism's one great success story.

Nevertheless, the Soviet Union stuck fast to their anti-intervention narrative. In his analysis of the Soviet archives, "Soviet Involvement in the Korean War: A New View from the Soviet-Era Archives," Mark O'Neill argues that this is because "the superpower confrontation of the Korean War was as much the result of historical accident, bad timing, and diplomatic blundering as it was calculation," and that the Soviet Union's resistance to taking credit for North Korea was because they genuinely didn't have a good sense of why or how things were happening, and were reluctant to put their name on a wild card like North Korea.

Nikolay Melteshinov

Nikolay Melteshinov was one of just a handful of Soviet soldiers who ended up on the frontlines of the Korean War – and, as far as I know, is the only one who wrote a memoir about it. Since the Soviet Union was maintaining plausible deniability about their role in the war, Melteshinov was supposed to avoid letting anyone know that he was a Soviet operative. He was undercover in the Chinese military, and saw first-hand what the Soviet forces were experiencing in the war. He comments, for example, that "at the time, the most modern aircraft, the F-86 Sabre, started to come off the assembly lines in American factories... The MiGs [Soviet planes] were inferior to Sabres in many respects. We helped our air forces as much as we could."

Melteshinov discusses the up-front experience of the war, from bragging about how many Sabres his division shot down, to telling about what happened after one North Korean pilot defected to the South:

> Americans then dropped leaflets on our positions, urging us to do the same. However, they were mistaken in their estimations. Soviet soldiers had very warm relationships with the Chinese and Korean fighters. On the first of October, the Chinese invited us to celebrate their holiday... and, on the first of May and the seventh of November, we invited them to our celebrations.

Perspectives: Chinese Veterans on the Korean War

The Korean War remains a rather contentious topic among veterans from China, as now, years later, it seems a bit difficult to tell what the purpose of the war was, and whether their suffering was for any real noble

117

cause. Unlike the Soviet Union, China has not declassified documents regarding the Korean War (because, unlike the Soviet Union, China has not collapsed). As many as four hundred thousand Chinese soldiers might have been killed in the conflicts (numbers are one of the things that we might learn from the documents once they're declassified), and for what reason? Propaganda told civilians that they were protecting their country from American imperialists, but were they really?

Zhang Zeshi, a veteran who spent time in a prisoner of war camp, says, "I regretted joining the war when I found out the US had no plan to invade China at that time." If the leaders had at least been honest about the war's purpose, Zhang might have felt differently, but as it is, he objects to the dishonesty of the war.

On the other hand, many Chinese veterans feel that they can and should be proud of their efforts in the war. After all, they were a people's army that stood up against the army of the United States, the much bigger and more powerful force. "We, PVA, are the world's first troops to defeat the US army... we successfully punished the US, the world's superpower, and made the Americans respect us," said Huang Zhao, who had joined the Chinese army when he was only fifteen years old to fight in Korea. Veterans like Huang argue that the outcome of the war were more beneficial for China's image than the causes were harmful for its people.

Refugees and the Chinese Border

China and North Korea share a border – a pretty long one, and one that's *significantly* less guarded than the Demilitarized Zone, which is North Korea's only other land border. Because of this, the border between North Korea and China is pretty much the go-to for anyone seeking to escape from North Korea.

Before and during the Korean War, most North Korean refugees made their escape into South Korea – estimates of almost seven and a half *hundred thousand* before the War, and six and a half hundred thousand during it. Moving north, into China, was a less favorable option, because most of these people were facing persecution under communism. The persecution was usually for their religion – communist regimes are generally *very* opposed to organized religion, especially Christianity. So moving into China would have been going out of the frying pan and into the fire.

However, when the border between North and South Korea was hardened into the DMZ in 1953, crossing it became a much bigger challenge, and the numbers dropped from hundreds of thousands to around, like *ten* in a year.

Suddenly, the people escaping North Korea weren't escaping communist ideology – they were escaping a totalitarian regime and a "nation of slavehood," and while China was hardly sunshine and roses, it looked a million times better than North Korea. Escaping via the Chinese border became a much more viable option.

Crossing the border is only one part of the challenge of escaping North Korea. If an escapee is captured, they will be imprisoned and possibly executed. Even worse, any family they leave behind could be subject to the same punishments, even if they didn't have anything to do with it.

Most people who escape via the Chinese border move to South Korea, or to western Europe or the Americas, rather than staying in China permanently. Although China is a big step up from the dictatorship of North Korea, it's still a North Korean ally, and much more likely to pass a refugee over to Kim Jong-un than South Korea or the United States might be.

China and North Korea Today

Today, in 2018, with the Soviet Union long-since dissolved, China is the one country that has a serious working relationship with North Korea. China's foreign aid to North Korea accounts about half of all its foreign aid, and is given directly to the city of Pyongyang in order to avoid United Nations sanctions. The relationship between these countries has been the source of massive controversy as tensions have escalated between North Korea and the United States, since the United States also has a major trade relationship with China.

However, in the last few years, even though China is maintaining its long-standing diplomatic relations with North Korea, they have started to pull back from their relationship. 46% of Chinese citizens have a negative view of their government's relationship with North Korea, with only 20% expressing a positive view, and 34% reporting mixed or neutral feelings.

China has supported recent sanctions against North Korea, and banned importing coal from them, which was North Korea's one big source of external income. United States president Donald Trump has encouraged China to sever all ties with North Korea in the wake of North Korea's nuclear tests and threats against both the United States and Japan. We'll have to wait and see how this relationship continues to develop over the next few years, as nuclear threats become even more serious and prominent.

RANDOM FACTS

1. In China, the Korean War is called "The War to Resist United States Aggression and Aid Korea."

2. India provided aid to both North and South Korea at various points in the war.

3. Some historians have suggested that the United States, General Douglas MacArthur sent troops into the northernmost parts of North Korea early in the war with the specific intention of stirring up civil unrest in China and reigniting the Chinese Civil War. It clearly did not work to his advantage.

4. The United States aerial reconnaissance forces did not detect the movement of Chinese forces because the Chinese People's Volunteer Army traveled only by night. The mountain ranges of China and North Korea offered them protection during the day.

5. According to Melteshinov, the Korean and Chinese military personnel called all Soviet soldiers by the title of "Captain," whether that was their official title or not.

6. Melteshinov also told humorous stories of the cultural sharing between Soviet and Chinese soldiers, who he called his "brothers in the building

of socialism." For example, he says, "the Chinese caught fish using pelicans. A hungry pelican was tied to a rope and its throat was restricted by a tight ring to prevent it from swallowing. The pelican would catch a fish, and the fisherman would take the fish from its mouth… we laughed together, but still, our soldiers caught more fish."

7. Although it was an open secret that the Soviet Union was sending soldiers to aid the North Korean forces, the Soviet Union only officially admitted it in the late 1970s.

8. The Chinese People's Volunteer Army used battle tactics that made their relatively small numbers appear much larger. They would attack flanking soldiers and get behind the enemy lines in order to make it seem like they were coming from all directions.

9. They also frequently attacked at night to continue to capitalize on the element of surprise.

10. Although the Chinese People's Volunteer Army was known for being strict and highly disciplined, it was actually a less strict force than previous Chinese armies. Communist Party members, rather than occupying privileged status, were punished more severely for infractions than non-Party members because it was seen as their responsibility to uphold the Communist Party's

honor. The army's regulations also forbid beating as a punishment, and was very strict about abuses of power within the army.

11. They also executed far fewer American Prisoners of War than the North Korean People's Army did.

12. Over the period since the Korean war, more women than men have escaped from North Korea into China. Many are trafficked to Chinese men, but many others have successful independent lives. Some scholars speculate that this is because women are more likely to acquire or consume non-North Korean media through the black market than men are, which interests them in outside life.

13. China is North Korea's biggest trade partner today. North Korea barely makes it into China's top 100.

14. China has been prompted to extend more sanctions against North Korea after North Korea captured several Chinese fishing vessels. This was seen as an act of very bad faith, and has damaged relations between the two countries.

15. Of all the countries of the world, China now has the most influence over North Korea, and so its sanctions have the most impact.

16. Perhaps oddly (considering that Russia has moved much further away from its communist roots than China has today), 19% of Russians view North

Korea positively and 37% view it negatively, compared to China's 20% positive and 46% negative view.

17. However, only 8% of all Russians polled in 2013 supported Russia aiding North Korea in a potential conflict.

18. A major source of anti-North Korea sentiment in modern Russia is the debt owed to Russia by North Korea. A deal signed in 2012 estimates that North Korea owes the former Soviet Union around eleven *billion* dollars.

19. The border between Russia and North Korea is Russia's shortest international border.

20. Russia was a popular destination for North Korean refugees who wanted to escape from North Korea's petty dictatorship but who still felt some adherence to ideals of communism. There is a significant Korean diaspora in the former Soviet Union today.

Test Yourself – Questions and Answers

1. What does PVA stand for?

   a. People of Vietnam and America
   b. People's Volunteer Army
   c. Prospective Vehicular Action

2. Who was Nikolay Melteshinov?

   a. A Soviet soldier in the Chinese army, who documented his experiences
   b. An ethnically Korean diplomat born in the Soviet Union, who negotiated on behalf of both countries during the armistice agreements
   c. A Soviet leader who opposed Soviet intervention in the Korean War and was executed due to pressure from Kim Il-sung

3. Which is true of Chinese veterans of the Korean War today?

   a. They object to the way the true purpose of the Korean War was hidden from Chinese citizens through propaganda
   b. They see their actions in the Korean War as a source of pride, because they successfully fought against the larger and better-equipped American forces
   c. Both these perspectives are true

4. What is the Korean War called in China?
   a. The War to Resist United States Aggression
   b. The War to Aid Korea
   c. The War to Resist United States Aggression and
      Aid Korea
5. When were the Soviet archives regarding the
   Korean War opened?
   a. The 1950s
   b. The 1990s
   c. They have not yet been opened

Answers

1. b
2. a
3. c
4. c
5. b

CHAPTER SIX

THE LEGACY OF
THE KOREAN WAR

Almost seventy years after North Korea crossed the 38th parallel into South Korea and war was declared, the world is still living in the shadow of the Korean War. But it doesn't feel like that. Some wars, like World War I, World War II, or the American Civil War, make themselves apparent every day, with dozens of film adaptations of their great stories, memorials scattered across the globe, and every student of a half-decent history class being expected to know at least the broad strokes. But the Korean War is different. The world isn't in its shadow because of how many people died, or how much changed about geopolitics. The world is living in its shadow because it is the war that will not end.

Daesong-dong and Living in the DMZ

Daesong-dong (sometimes Romanized as Taesong-dong) is the only South Korean town to exist within the

Demilitarized Zone. It is only one mile away from Kijong-dong, a North Korean village in the DMZ, making it the closest South Korean town to any North Korean town.

Living in Daesong-dong makes residents a kind of hybrid nationality: they are South Korean citizens, but they are under the administration of the United Nations Command, which is in charge of the Demilitarized Zone. This means that Daesong-dong residents have special privileges and restrictions, compared to other South Korean residents. For example, they are subject to normal South Korean laws, but they do not have to pay taxes. They can vote and receive public education like all South Koreans, but they do not have to participate in the military or any national defence projects (living in the DMZ is military enough, really). The main economy of Daesong-dong is farming. All residents are given large plots of farm land, and their farming wages are higher than those elsewhere in the country.

But living in the DMZ isn't a bed of roses (not that you'd assume it would be). North Korean soldiers are allowed to enter the village – they can't bring weapons, but we all saw how well that worked in Operation Paul Bunyan. Because of this, there are very strict limitations to protect civilians' safety. If anyone wants to visit the village, even family members of residence, they must state that they are coming two weeks in advance, so that they can be provided with a military escort. Everyone must be off the streets at 11 PM, and there is a mandatory headcount every night to make sure no one has been abducted.

Daesong-dong Versus Kijong-dong

Besides the weirdness that comes from living in what is essentially "no man's land" between warring states, Daesong-dong has a bizarre rivalry with its North Korean counterpart, Kijong-dong. Since they are only a mile apart, the towns are within sight of each other. This has made them the subject of petty national competitions, like each side is trying to show the other, with this one little town, how great their side is.

Kijong-dong is so explicit in these tactics that it's known as "Propaganda Village" (the alternative official North Korean name for it is *pyonghwachon* or "Peace Village"). North Korea insists that the village is built around a collective farm (a classic communist model), and that there are two hundred families, a kindergarten, a hospital, and primary and secondary schools. But it's not quite clear who they think they're fooling, because South Korea, including the citizens of Daesong-dong, insist that the village is uninhabited and hasn't had anyone living in it since the '50s, when, they claim, it was built for the express purpose of making the country look good. This is completely believable, as North Korea frequently uses the tactic of establishing "showpiece cities" or installations that are meant to make their country look good to outsiders while not addressing the issues within. Pyongyang is another city like this.

In the 1980s, these two towns were part of a bizarre competition in which the national governments competed to build the tallest flagpoles in the world. Daesong-dong started with a 323-foot tall flagpole, and Kijong-dong retaliated with a 525-foot tall flagpole hoisting a flag that weighed almost six hundred pounds.

East Germany and West Germany as an Analogy to Korea

We mentioned way back in Chapter One that the technique that the Soviet Union and United States used for dividing up Korean territory after World War II was very similar to how they divided German territory: the Soviet Union took responsibility for reconstructing one half, and the United States took responsibility for reconstructing the other.

When the Korean War hit, there was widespread panic in the western parts of the Soviet Union that people in Germany might get *ideas*, and that a civil war might ensue there. Both the eastern, communist side, and the western, capitalist side were terrified that the other might try to invade and establish their own government. However, this didn't happen (at least, not until the Berlin Wall came down in 1989, and it was all pretty much over by then). This may have been because, unlike Korea, Germany was flanked on all sides by countries who had a vested interest in the outcome, one way or the other, and they knew that if they tried to start a civil war, they would immediately be invaded by one of their many neighbors – who were all still a little on-edge from the whole Third Reich thing.

M*A*S*H

One of the most significant media portrayals of the Korean War is the television show M*A*S*H, named over the MASH Mobile Army Surgical Hospitals which were developed and deployed during the Korean War to provide more immediate relief for wounded soldiers.

M*A*S*H was based on a movie, which was based on a book called MASH: A Noel About Three Army Doctors by Richard Hooker, written in 1968 – fifteen years after the Korean War ended. The show M*A*S*H was different from many previous depictions of the big-scale wars of the twentieth century. It was a humorous depiction of war, showing humor as a coping mechanism for the brutal and absurd reality of war. This sort of depiction gained popularity in the later part of the twentieth century, as people simply seemed to get burned out on the dark, brutal, "the world is cold and unfeeling" depictions of war that characterized the interwar period.

The Manchurian Candidate

The other really significant film depiction of the Korean War is the 1962 film *The Manchurian Candidate*, based on the 1959 novel of the same title. *The Manchurian Candidate* uses the Korean War as the setting for a thriller about a politician being brainwashed into becoming a communist assassin. In the film, an American Sergeant is captured and taken to Manchuria, the part of communist China that borders on North Korea, where he is involved in the brainwashing experiments. The brainwashing is assisted back in America by a North Korean secret agent, who implants false memories about the politician being a hero, in order to get their man into power. It's a classic piece of Cold War anxiety, straight out of the era of McCarthyism.

But even *The Manchurian Candidate*, with its Cold War sensibilities and its explicit Asian setting, has been overshadowed by a 2004 remake that completely strips out the Korean War, using instead a post-9/11 setting to highlight the same anxiety that was felt in the Cold War. The "Manchurian" of the title becomes something of an artifact, as the 2004 film has nothing to do with Manchuria, but instead the villains are part of a corporation called Manchurian Global. The prominence of the remake shows a vast shift in anxieties after the Cold War ended, and especially after the United States' post-9/11 "War on Terror" brought so many similar concerns back into the public mind.

Why Aren't There More Movies about the Korean War?

If the two most significant portrayals of the Korean War are a movie that was overshadowed by its 2004 non-Korean-War-related remake, and a comedy about medics (rather than the traditional soldier heroes), you might be wondering now – why is it that the Korean War doesn't seem to be a very popular setting for films? When the Vietnam War and World War II, which flank the Korean War, are both wildly popular media goldmines... what's wrong with the Korean War?

That's a complicated question, and there are many potential answers. For one thing, it may simply be a case of burnout. The twentieth century has basically been a nonstop stream of wars from 1914 onwards, and some of them just have to be more popular than others. We've got World War I, World War II, the generic Cold War, Vietnam, and the War on Terror to fill up our media – can we really find time for the Korean War, when many of the themes from an American perspective are better covered by generic Cold War or Vietnam?

Another issue may be race – the Korean War was a war between Koreans and Koreans, and let's be real:

Hollywood just doesn't have that many Korean actors. Hollywood is also not traditionally *super* interested in portraying the complex intra-political struggles of other nations, and so there may be some reluctance around diving in to the political context that made the Korean War possible.

Finally, there may be just a little anxiety about portraying the Korean War on film because it's still going on. The peace is uneasy – more so than ever in the last few years – and creators may simply be reluctant to put it on film because they don't want to jinx what peace there is on the Korean peninsula.

All of these reasons, and undoubtedly many more, are factors in why the Korean War may not be as popular a setting as other wars for media. What do you think the reason is?

North Korean Propaganda

You know who makes *tons* of films about the Korean War? North Korea. North Korean propaganda films are as numerous as American ones are scarce, and like all North Korean propaganda that we've looked at, their ultimate goal is to show how North Korea came up from behind and survived the American imperialist threat. Kim Il-sung wrote an opera (allegedly, it's always hard to know what Kim Il-sung actually did, and what people just say that he did) called *Sea of Blood* that is set during the Japanese occupation of Korea in the 1930s, but the themes of Korean nationalism and *Juche* are still heavily alluding to the Korean War.

Dozens of other films and television spots have been developed by the North Korean propaganda offices in order to display how the Korean people braved American imperialism. However, for obvious reasons, most of these films don't make it to a western audience – North Korea isn't exactly concerned about spreading them to America, and most Americans don't particularly want to watch them.

The Interview

Speaking of films that people don't want to watch, in 2014, Sony Pictures released the film *The Interview*, a comedy about an assassination plot against Kim Jong-un… but not without serious resistance. While you certainly don't see anyone trying to stop Quentin Tarantino from making a film about killing Hitler, or Ben Affleck from making a film about killing Osama Bin Laden, there was a genuine effort to stop *The Interview* from getting made.

Right before its release date, Sony Pictures was hacked into and threatened with retaliation if they decided to release the movie. Sony withdrew the film, but then was met with massive criticism from within the United States for bowing to what many viewed as a terrorist threat. President Barack Obama even criticized Sony for their decision, saying that they should stand by their art and allow the government to handle the threat, if there was anything to it (which, it seems, most people suspected there really wasn't). Reluctantly, Sony released the film to any theatre that would run it.

As it turned out, North Korea definitely didn't have the power to do anything about the release of *The Interview*. It was all bluster and no action, and neither Sony Pictures nor the directors or actors became targets of further attacks. However, this shows how dedicated North Korea is to keeping up a positive image of their leaders – even though everyone who might have seen the movie would certainly already have a negative view of Kim Jong-un, without James Franco's help.

Education in South Korea

After the Korean War, South Korea put a focus on rebuilding and modernizing the country, not unlike what happened with the Korean Empire at the turn of the twentieth century, like we saw in Chapter One. The main focus of South Korea's reforming and rebuilding tactics was reforming the Korean education system.

Prior to the Korean War, both under Japanese occupation and in the inter-war period of Soviet and American oversight, education had been available only to the elite children of South Korea. But in the period after the Korean War, the South Korean government realized that the only way they would be able to compete in a modern economy as a fully-fledged capitalist nation would be to develop a world-class education system. They wanted their students to be the envy of the entire world.

The South Korean education system is notoriously rigorous. Students attend conventional classes from 8 in the morning to 4 in the afternoon every weekday, but that's only the beginning. From 4 to as late as 8 PM, students review their work in study hall periods, and then, until 10 or as late as midnight (or later), they go to *hagwons*, private academies that are meant to fill in gaps in their public education. All of this is in preparation for a massive university entrance exam, which South Korean kids take in their final year of high school, which determines what universities they can go to.

Is the South Korean Education System *Juche*?

In South Korea, education is seen as a great equalizer. The whole system is designed to be highly meritocratic: if you work hard (in theory) you score well on the test, and then you get into the top schools, which guarantee you high-paying jobs. Unlike the United States, you can't get into the top schools just because your family has a lot of money and you can afford tuition. The principle behind this is that nobody should be stuck with a poorly-paying job because their family couldn't afford to send them to a good university. It should be all about the work that they do to earn that university position.

This emphasis on individual work to overcome economic hardship might sound a little familiar. It might sound like the kind of thing that the North Korean philosophy would support. The focus on abandoning class background, that all people are as worthy as their work, and the certain individualism within a highly structured society all look a lot like the North Korean ideology of *Juche*.

This is not to say that the South Korean education system is somehow "bad" just because it looks kind of like what the North Koreans say that they're doing (remember, the ideology of *Juche* is pretty different from the reality of North Korena life). Quite the contrary: the South Korean education system is demonstrably excellent, at least if you measure excellence by the system's ability to create top-of-the-world scholars.

What this similarity does show is that the idea of *Juche* didn't spring out of nowhere. It's not just communism with a thin veneer of Korean ethnocentrism smacked on top. It comes out of a distinct context, and, when it's not being applied by a totalitarian dictator, that ideology can actually be used for good instead of evil.

North Korea's Nuclear Program

North Korea's experiments into nuclear weaponry have been all over the news for the last year. In fact, they've been all over the news since Kim Jong-un, who had been struggling to step out from under the very long shadow cast by his father, Kim Jong-Il, and the even longer one cast by his grandfather, Kim Il-sung, declared that nuclear weapons were a North Korean national priority.

Prior to 2003, North Korea was part of a treaty called the Treaty on the Non-Proliferation of Nuclear Weapons, which was created to promote the peaceful use of nuclear energy. But in 2003, Kim Jong-Il withdrew North Korea from the treaty, and since then, the country has been committed to developing nuclear weapons.

North Korea's first nuclear test was an underground nuclear explosion in 2006, and by 2009, they were determined to have become a "fully fledged nuclear power." In the nine years since that statement, North Korea has continued to detonate test bombs of increasingly significant size.

ICBMs

Last year, in 2017, North Korea conducted their most significant nuclear program-related tests yet, when they launched two ICBMs, or inter-continental ballistic missiles. One of these missiles was powerful enough that, if launched towards the United States, it would be able to strike the continent.

North Korea's ICBMs have reawakened anxiety about North Korea in the American consciousness. While it would be uncharitable and untrue to say that Americans generally weren't too worried about the possibility of North Korea bombing one of its neighbors, like South Korea or Japan, it is also true that, of course, most Americans are significantly more worried about a bomb reaching their own homes. A potential war with North Korea is now one of the main political issues on people's minds in the United States.

Donald Trump

In late 2016, Donald Trump was elected president of the United States with an outspoken and inflammatory rhetoric and a tendency to make political issues into personal ones. Trump has spent the first year of his presidency writing inflammatory things about North Korea on social media, especially Twitter (his platform of choice). He threatened North Korea by saying, "North Korea best not make any more threats to the United States... they will be met with fire and fury like the world has never seen" in a summer speech. In September, Trump resorted to name-calling when he said, "Just heard Foreign Minister of North Korea speak at U.N. If he echoes thoughts of Little Rocket

Man, they won't be around much longer!" And even more recently, in January 2018, he was accused of reducing the threat of nuclear war to "a literal dick-measuring contest" when he tweeted, "North Korean Leader Kim Jong Un just stated that the 'Nuclear Button is on his desk at all times.' Will someone from his depleted and food starved regime please inform him that I, too, have a Nuclear Button, but it is a much bigger & more powerful one than his, and my button works!"

Trump has been heavily criticized for being undiplomatic, and many people are terrified that his intentionally inflammatory comments will spur North Korea even more strongly towards nuclear war.

The Pyeongchang Olympics

Despite – or, his supporters would say, because of – Trump's aggressive attitude towards North Korea, a breakthrough recently occurred in North Korean/South Korean diplomatic relations. The 2018 Winter Olympics took place in the county of Pyeongchang, South Korea. This massive, multinational sporting event led to the first high-level diplomatic talks between North and South Korean officials in more than two years.

In these talks, North Korea said that they were interested in participating in the games. Less than two months later, they made their showing at the Olympics with an opening ceremony march where North and

South Korea marched together, and a unified women's hockey team. Kim Yo-jong, Kim Jong-un's younger sister, attended the games, where she also had a meeting with the South Korean president Moon Jae-in. This was the first time since the Korean War that a member of the Kim family visited South Korea.

The Pyeongchang Olympics have been hailed by many as a step towards Korean unification – but not everyone sees that as a good thing. Some critics have said that the efforts towards unification are giving tacit approval to North Korea's totalitarian regime. Protestors called it the "Pyongyang Olympics," indicating their belief that this was all a strategic propaganda move by North Korea to make their country look good, just like the entire existence of Pyongyang is, and that South Korea was just buckling under pressure from North Korea.

Is there Hope for Korea?

In spite of protesters' doubts, which may very well be well-founded, the Pyeongchang Olympics mark a turning point in the history of the Korean War. It may be that we are standing at the end of the Korean War, and by the time you've finished this book, Korea may be reunified. Or it's possible that the North Korean presence in Pyeongchang was just a public relations move, and that North Korea is about to return to the fight with a vengeance. At this time, it's impossible to know.

After reading this book, you might be better equipped to understand what happened in Korea in 1950, and how those events are still affecting the Korean peninsula today. No matter what happens next, whether it's peace, war, or just continued armistice, you are now armed with knowledge. So, next time you see an aggressive tweet from Donald Trump, or hear that North Korea has launched another test missile, or hear that conversations are happening between North and South Korea, you will be just a bit better prepared to think about the question… is there hope for Korea?

RANDOM FACTS

1. One of the major reasons the Korean War dragged on and the post-war negotiations were so messy was simply poor communication between the two sides, and *especially* between the allies. Washington and Beijing had a *very* hard time communicating with each other, and minor issues ballooned into massive ones.

2. Compared to many of the wars that we've covered in our war facts series, like World War II, the Vietnam War, and the American Civil War, the Korean War has not been a favorite source of pop cultural artifacts like movies or video games. Its relative obscurity has led to some people calling it "the forgotten war."

3. A better reason to call the Korean War "the forgotten war" is that many people seem to forget it's still going on.

4. The Korean War was the first time that the category of drugs known as amphetamines were used. Some soldiers mixed amphetamines with heroin and injected the mixture into their arms to keep themselves awake during long, cold, and uncomfortable battle periods. Amphetamines are extremely dangerous and highly addictive drugs,

and many Korean War soldiers remained addicted after they returned to the United States.

5. North Korean refugees often have difficulty adapting to life in South Korea or other capitalist nations. As brutal as the communist regime is, capitalist society has its own brutalities. Many refugees struggle to come to terms with the massive disparities in wealth in capitalist systems, and some feel like they are being exploited just as much – just by different exploiters. However, many have gone on to have extremely successful lives, either integrating into "normal" society, or taking on activist roles against totalitarianism.

6. Kijong-dong's 525-foot tall flagpole was indeed the tallest in the world when it was built, but it has now been outstripped by the National Flag Square in Baku, Azerbaijan, the Dushanbe Flagpole in Tajikistan, and the Jeddah Flagpole in Saudi Arabia.

7. The final episode of the show *M*A*S*H*, "Goodbye, Farewell, and Amen," was the most-watched television episode at the time.

8. South Korean students who score in the top percentiles of the university entrance exam, and get into the top South Korean universities, have access to much better jobs than their lower-scoring peers. However, they will also be paid more for

whatever job they do. Even if they're working an entry-level position, their degree will earn them a bonus.

9. North Korea appealed to China for help with its nuclear program, but China refused to offer assistance.

10. In addition to trading coal with China, much of North Korea's import market comes from its drug trade. Marijuana is legal in North Korea, and exported to nearby countries. There is also a thriving trade in counterfeit pharmaceuticals, which are sold on the black market into China and Japan, as well as within the country.

11. Marijuana is not even legally classified as a drug in North Korea. This surprises many Americans, because the sanctions against marijuana in the United States are so harsh, and have been for decades. This is one place where the United States is much more strict than North Korea!

12. According to the North Korean office of propaganda, Kim Jong-Il sank 11 holes-in-one the first time he played golf.

13. North Korea's first missile program was developed in the 1970s, with the help of the Soviet Union, when the conflict between North and South Korea was still part of a bigger world-wide Cold War.

14. Kim Jong-un's older brother, Kim Jong-nam, was assassinated on February 13, 2017. He had previously been exiled from North Korea in 2003.

15. In 2001, Kim Jong-nam (age 30 at the time) attempted to visit Tokyo Disneyland with a fake passport, and was caught. Prior to this event, he was the heir of the North Korean regime. Although he claimed that he fell out of favor due to his criticisms, many people have speculated that the real reason Kim Jong-nam was exiled from the country was this embarrassing incident.

16. Neither South Korea nor Japan officially recognize North Korea as an independent state.

17. North Korea doesn't consider itself an independent state, either, but simply the part of Korea that's not under American imperialist control. This is why the push for reunification is so significant from both sides.

18. In 2012, North Korean archeologists announced that they had discovered the hidden lair of a two-thousand-year-old unicorn ridden by King Tyongmyung in the first century BC.

19. In 2017, an American student who went on a tour of North Korea died due to an "unknown injury" that happened while he was being held against his will. The student was held in North Korea after he was accused of trying to steal a poster, and died

more than a year later. His name was Otto Warmbier, and he was 22 years old when he died.

20. In spite of this, if you're still interested, it continues to be possible to take a tour of North Korea. Various tour companies arrange both group and individual tours, where visitors can choose which sights they want to see, and are accompanied by escorts to cultural and natural landmarks. However, Otto Warmbier's death and other incidents like it have led most leaders to advise against taking these trips. If you do choose to travel to North Korea, you must be prepared to take the risk that you will be detained and possibly not survive. Despite the risk, travel to North Korea remains surprisingly popular for seasoned travelers.

Test Yourself – Questions and Answers

1. What did President Obama say about Sony Pictures' decision not to release *The Interview*?

    a. That their decision was wise, because the United States shouldn't do anything to antagonize North Korea unnecessarily.
    b. That their decision was bad, because they were allowing a dictator to censor art.
    c. Obama did not comment on the film *The Interview*.

2. Which one of these is *not* a nickname for the North Korean town of Kijong-dong?

    a. Peace Village, because North Korea wanted to use it to display the best qualities of their country.
    b. Propaganda Village, because North Korea wanted to use it to *dishonestly* portray good qualities of their country that don't exist.
    c. Pot Village, because North Korea is active in the marijuana market.

3. Which of these is *not* a rule for the residents of the South Korean town of Daesong-dong?

    a. They must be prepared to shoot a North Korean soldier on sight
    b. They are allowed to attend South Korean schools
    c. They must be home every night by 11 PM

4. Which important North Korean diplomat attended the Pyeongchang Winter Olympics in 2018?

   a. Kim Jong-un
   b. Moon Jae-in
   c. Kim Yo-jong

5. What happened in 2003?

   a. North Korea withdrew from the Treaty on the Non-Proliferation of Nuclear Weapons
   b. North Korea attended the Olympics with South Korea
   c. Kim Jong-un assumed office as the leader of North Korea

Answers

1. b
2. c
3. a
4. c
5. a

The End

Don't forget to check out the
previous books in this series:

The World War II Trivia Book

The Vietnam War Trivia Book

The American Civil War Trivia Book

DON'T FORGET YOUR
FREE BOOKS

GET THEM FOR FREE ON
WWW.TRIVIABILL.COM

MORE BOOKS BY BILL O'NEILL

I hope you enjoyed this book and learned something new. Please feel free to check out some of my previous books on **Amazon**.

CPSIA information can be obtained
at www.ICGtesting.com
Printed in the USA
BVHW061758040222
627989BV00008B/406